Crossing
the TOEIC Bridge®
−New Edition−

Shiho Hayashi

Harumi Nishida

Brian Covert

Asahi Press

音声再生アプリ「リスニング・トレーナー」を使った 音声ダウンロード

朝日出版社開発のアプリ、「リスニング・トレーナー（リストレ）」を使えば、教科書の音声を
スマホ、タブレットに簡単にダウンロードできます。どうぞご活用ください。

◉ アプリ【リスニング・トレーナー】の使い方

《アプリのダウンロード》

App Store または Google Play から
「リスニング・トレーナー」のアプリ
（無料）をダウンロード

App Storeは
こちら▶

Google Playは
こちら▶

《アプリの使い方》

① アプリを開き「コンテンツを追加」をタップ
② 画面上部に【15667】を入力しDoneをタップ

音声ストリーミング配信 》》》

この教科書の音声は、
右記ウェブサイトにて
無料で配信しています。

https://text.asahipress.com/free/english/

はじめに

　TOEIC® Listening & Reading Test（以降、TOEIC®テスト）は、日常生活やビジネスシーンで活かせる英語のリスニング力やリーディング力を測定するテストです。IIBC一般財団法人国際ビジネスコミュニケーション協会によると、2018年度には約3,100の企業・団体・学校がTOEIC®テストを採用し、個人での申し込みを合わせ、年間約246万人が受験しています。現在では、目標スコアを設定し、授業の一環として、TOEIC®テスト対策を行う大学が増えてきました。また、企業の人員採用や海外部門要員の選定、さらには昇進・昇格の要件として活用されるといったように、このテストの需要は年々増えています。

　一方、TOEIC Bridge® Listening & Reading Tests（以降、TOEIC Bridge®テスト）は、TOEIC®テストのための架け橋として、TOEIC®テストよりも「易しくて」「日常的で身近な」「時間の短い」初級学習者向けのテストを求める声にこたえるべく、TOEIC®プログラムを開発した機関のETSにより制作されました。TOEIC Bridge®テストは、大学だけでなく、中学、高等学校でも英語力を測るものさしとして幅広く使われています。

　本テキストは、TOEIC®テストの受験経験がなく、英語学習を一からやり直し、まずはTOEIC Bridge®テストの対策から始めてみたいという学習者をターゲットにしています。そして、最終目標は、TOEIC Bridge®テストで高得点を取るだけでなく、現在広く活用されている、TOEIC®テストでも役立つ基礎的な英語力と知識を身につけることを目標としています。

　本テキストのユニット1から5までは、TOEIC Bridge®テストのすべてのパートの問題を配置し、ユニット6以降は、各ユニットにTOEIC®テストのすべてのパートの問題を配置しています。また、テスト問題に頻繁に出てくる語彙を強化するために、リスニング・セクションとリーディング・セクションの前には、語彙をチェックするための問題を設けています。巻末には各ユニットで出てきた重要語句のVocabulary Check Listを載せています。各パートの英文は、実際のTOEIC®テストでよく見られるものであり、英語としてナチュラルな表現を意識しました。

　問題を解くことで、英語に対する感性を研ぎ澄ませてもらいたいと思います。本テキストを隅から隅まで活用することにより、皆さんの英語力が向上し、あわせてTOEIC Bridge®テストとTOEIC®テストのスコアが向上すれば、これに勝る喜びはありません。

　本書を刊行するにあたり、編集および発行段階では朝日出版社の朝日英一郎様には大変お世話になりました。また、他の編集部の皆様にも各段階で大変お世話になりました。ここに感謝申し上げます。

2020年10月

著者

本書について

本書の構成

　本書は実際のTOEIC Bridge® L&R Tests と TOEIC® L&R Testに準拠した問題とともに、語彙の練習問題や文法説明を設けています。テスト対策をしつつも、英語の基礎的な知識を身につけることを目標に据えています。

　本書の構成は以下のとおりです。

Unit 1 から Unit 5 まで

◆ **Before Listening・Vocabulary check**（語彙問題）

　Listening Test のPART 1 からPART 4 で出てくる重要語句を理解しましょう。

◆ **TOEIC Bridge® L&R練習問題 LISTENING PART 1: Four Pictures**（画像選択問題）

　句や文を聞いて、4つの絵の中から、その句や文を最もよく表す絵を選びましょう。

◆ **TOEIC Bridge® L&R練習問題 LISTENING PART 2: Question-Response**（応答問題）

　質問や発言を聞いて、4つの選択肢の中から、応答として最も適切なものを選びましょう。

◆ **TOEIC Bridge® L&R練習問題 LISTENING PART 3: Conversation**（会話問題）

　2者の短い会話を聞いて、会話に関する2つの設問に解答しましょう。（本番の試験では看板やお知らせなどの簡単な補足図表を参照する問題もあります。）

◆ **TOEIC Bridge® L&R練習問題 LISTENING PART 4: Talk**（説明文問題）

　1人の話し手による短いメッセージやお知らせなどを聞いて、その内容に関する2つの設問に解答しましょう。（本番の試験では、看板やお知らせなどの簡単な補足図表を参照する問題もあります。）

◆ **Before Reading・Vocabulary check**（語彙問題）

　Reading Test のPART 1 から3に出てくる重要語句を理解しましょう。

◆ **Grammar**

　文法についての基礎知識を身につけましょう。

◆ **Practice**

　前のページのGrammar で学んだことが理解できているかを確認するために、まずは簡単な問題にチャレンジしてみましょう。

◆ **TOEIC Bridge® L&R練習問題 READING PART 1: Sentence Completion**（短文穴埋め問題）

　語や句が1カ所抜けている文を読んで、それを完成させるのに最も適当な選択肢を選びましょう。

◆ **TOEIC Bridge® L&R練習問題 READING PART 2: Text Completion**（長文穴埋め問題）

　語や句または文が3カ所抜けている文章を読んで、それを完成させるのに最も適切な選択肢を選びましょう。

◆ **TOEIC Bridge® L&R練習問題 READING PART 3: Reading Comprehension**（読解問題）

　1つの文書を読んで、それに関する3つの設問に解答しましょう。

◆ **Before Listening・Vocabulary check**（語彙問題）
　Part 1 から Part 4 で出てくる重要語句を理解しましょう。

◆ **TOEIC® L&R 練習問題 Part 1: Photographs**（写真描写問題）
　写真を見て英文を聞き、英語の聴解力を身につけましょう。

◆ **TOEIC® L&R 練習問題 Part 2: Question-Response**（応答問題）
　文字情報に頼らず、音声情報だけで英語を聴き取れるようにしましょう。

◆ **TOEIC® L&R 練習問題 Part 3: Conversation**（会話問題）
　会話をとおして英語の聴解力を身につけるとともに、会話でよく使われる表現を身につけましょう。

◆ **TOEIC® L&R 練習問題 Part 4: Talk**（説明文問題）
　説明文を聞き、より長い英語を聞き取れるようにしましょう。

◆ **Before Reading・Vocabulary check**（語彙問題）
　Part 5 から Part 7 で出てくる重要語句を理解しましょう。

◆ **Grammar**（文法説明）
　文法についての基礎知識を身につけましょう。

◆ **Practice**
　前のページの Grammar で学んだことが理解できているかを確認するために、まずは簡単な問題にチャレンジしてみましょう。

◆ **TOEIC® L&R 練習問題 Part 5: Incomplete Sentences**（短文穴埋め問題）
　文法問題をとおして、英語の文法や語彙の知識を増やしましょう。

◆ **TOEIC® L & R 練習問題 Part 6: Text Completion**（長文穴埋め問題）
　長文空所問題をとおして、英語の読解力を身につけるとともに、文法や語彙の知識を増やしましょう。

◆ **TOEIC® L&R 練習問題 Part 7: Single Passages**（1つの文書）/ **Multiple Passages**（複数の文書）
　様々な英文テキストを読み、問題に答えることで、英語の読解力を身につけましょう。

本書の使い方

　本書は Unit 1 から Unit 14 まで 14 のテーマに基づいて問題が作られています。まずは、Unit 1 から Unit 5 までの TOEIC Bridge® L&R Tests に準拠した問題から始めて、その後、Unit 6 以降の TOEIC® L&R Test 形式の問題に取り組んでください。

　各ユニットのリスニング問題とリーディング問題を解く前に、語彙問題によって語彙力の増強を図ってください。リスニング問題を解いた後に、音声データを活用して、英文の読み方と意味の両方を理解するようにしましょう。また各ユニットのリーディング問題を解く前には、文法説明をよく読んで理解し、文法の基礎的な知識を身につけるようにしてください。

　巻末には、この教科書で使われている重要語句の一覧をユニットごとに載せています。学習が終わってから、語彙が身についたかどうかを確認するための語彙リストとして活用してください。

TOEIC Bridge® L&R Tests の形式について

　TOEIC Bridge® L&R Test はリスニング（25 分間・50 問）、リーディング（35 分間・50 問）、合計 1 時間で 100 問に答えるマークシート方式の一斉客観テストです。

　テストは英文のみで構成されており、和文英訳・英文和訳といった設問はありません。解答方法の指示も英文のみです。出題形式は毎回同じで、解答はすべて問題用紙とは別の解答用紙にマークシート（正しいと思われる解答番号を選択して黒く塗りつぶす）方式で記入します。

テスト問題の構成

Listening Test （25 分間・50 問） 問題形式により 4 つのパートに分かれています。	
PART 1 （6 問）	**画像選択問題（Four Pictures）** 句や文を聞いて、4 つの絵の中から、その句や文を最もよく表す絵を選びましょう。人、場所、物、行動などの簡単な説明を理解する能力が求められます。
PART 2 （20 問）	**応答問題（Question-Response）** 質問や発言を聞いて、4 つの選択肢の中から、応答として最も適切なものを選びましょう。短い対話を理解できること、質問や発言に対する適切な応答が理解できることが求められます。
PART 3 （10 問）	**会話問題（Conversations ）** 2 者の短い会話を聞いて、会話に関する 2 つの設問に解答しましょう。看板やお知らせなどの簡単な補足図表を参照する問題もあります。短い会話を理解し、会話における主題、話し手の意図、詳細、示唆を理解する能力が求められます。
PART 4 （14 問）	**説明文問題（Talks）** 1 人の話し手による短いメッセージやお知らせなどを聞いて、その内容に関する 2 つの設問に解答しましょう。看板やお知らせなどの簡単な補足図表を参照する問題もあります。短いトークを理解し、そのトークにおける主題、話し手の意図、詳細、示唆を理解する能力が求められます。
Reading Test （35 分間・50 問） 問題形式により 3 つのパートに分かれています。	
PART 1 （15 問）	**短文穴埋め問題（Sentence Completion）** 語や句が 1 カ所抜けている文を読んで、それを完成させるのに最も適当な選択肢を選びましょう。語彙知識や文法知識が求められます。
PART 2 （15 問）	**長文穴埋め問題（Text Completion）** 語や句または文が 3 カ所抜けている文章を読んで、それを完成させるのに最も適切な選択肢を選びましょう。語彙知識や文法知識が求められます。また、短い文章の構成を理解する能力が求められます。

	読解問題 （Reading Comprehension）
PART 3 （20問）	1つの文書を読んで、それに関する2つか3つの設問に解答しましょう。看板や予定表などの文章構造ではない文書を理解できること、指示や説明、短く簡単な通信文を理解できることが求められます。また、お知らせ、手紙、インスタントメッセージなどの情報的で叙述的な短い文章を理解する能力も求められます。

参考文献：

『TOEIC Bridge® 公式ガイドブック：4技能対応』

一般財団法人 国際ビジネスコミュニケーション協会 （pp.18-19）

発行年月：2019年4月

TOEIC Bridge® L&R Tests の結果について

　テスト結果は合格・不合格ではなく、リスニング15～50点、リーディング15～50点、テストスコア30～100点の1点刻みで表示されます。このスコアは正答数そのままの素点（Raw Score）ではなく、スコアの同一化（Equating）と呼ばれる統計処理によって算出された換算点（Scaled Score）です。取得したスコアにより自分の英語能力を知ることができます。次の「スコアレンジ別評価一覧」をご覧ください。

Score Range Descriptors （スコアレンジ別評価一覧）

リスニングテスト	
39～50点	このスコアレンジに該当する受験者は一般的に、つながりのある文と多少複雑な構造を含む、短い会話やトークを理解できる。暗示されている意味や抽象的な概念を理解できることもある。一般的に、よく使われる語彙およびいくつかの複雑な文と文法構造を理解することができる。また一般的には、仕事やその他の身近な場面に関する具体的なトピックを理解でき、またそれらに関する抽象的な概念を理解できることもある。また暗示された意味のいくつかを理解でき、短い文書に記載された情報と、会話や短いトークに含まれる事柄とを関連付けることも可能である。身近でかつ必要なトピックであれば、フォーマルな話し言葉とカジュアルな話し言葉を理解できる。
26～38点	このスコアレンジに該当する受験者は一般的に、短い文と限られた範囲の文法構造を理解することができる。身近なトピックに関する短い話のやりとりを理解することができる。一般的に、明瞭かつゆっくりと話された発話を理解することができる。また通常、キーワード、定型の句や表現、比較的短い一文程度の発話を理解することができる。一般的に、身近なトピックや日課のような決まったことに関する話し言葉を理解し、人、家族、買い物、場所、仕事に関する簡単な説明や情報を理解することができる。多くの場合、簡単な文と文法構造を理解することができ、時として複雑な文章と文法構造を理解できることもある。時には、暗示されている意味を理解することができる。

16〜25点	このスコアレンジに該当する受験者は一般的に、ゆっくりと話された単語、簡単なフレーズ、身近なトピックに関する短い文を理解できることもある。明瞭かつ非常にゆっくりと話された短い発話を理解することができる。一般的に、よく使われる語彙が用いられていれば、短い定型表現や簡単な文、文法構造を理解することができる。身近なトピックにおいて、予測しやすい短いメッセージや指示を理解することができる。一度に一文ずつであれば、連続していない発話を理解できる。
15点	このスコアレンジに該当する受験者は、明瞭かつ非常にゆっくりと話された、いくつかの単語、非常に簡単なフレーズ、多少の短い文を理解できる。数字や曜日のような単語を理解できる受験者もいる。また質問や発言が予測の範囲内で、一度に1フレーズずつ話された場合に理解できる受験者もいる。非常に簡単な文法構造と、身近なトピックに関してよく使われる語彙で構成される文を理解できることもある。

リーディングテスト	
45〜50点	このスコアレンジに該当する受験者は、個人的、公的、あるいは身近な職場での場面で、さまざまな形式の短い文書を理解することができる。一般的に、フォーマル、インフォーマルな形式で書かれたウェブページ、手紙、記事のような、よく使われるさまざまな文書を理解することができる。また、英語で書かれた短い文書の基本的な構成を知っており、その知識を用いて文書を理解することができる。具体的なトピックに関する語彙を理解でき、日常生活についての抽象的なトピックに関する語彙を理解できることもある。さまざまな文法構造を知っており、複雑な文と構造を理解する力を身に付けつつある。複数の文にわたって情報を関連付けることができる。全体の意味、目的、多くの詳細を理解することができる。時には直接ではなく暗に示されている意味を理解することもできる。
34〜44点	このスコアレンジに該当する受験者は一般的に、よく使われる語彙と基本的な文法構造で書かれた短い文書を理解することができる。また、身近なトピックを説明する簡単な言葉を理解することができる。一般的に、短く簡単に書かれた文書を理解することができる。eメール、手紙、ウェブページなど、さまざまな形式の文書の全体的な意味を理解することができる。英語で書かれた文書の基本的な構成を知りつつあり、時にはその知識に基づいて文書を理解することができる。通常は、家族、買い物、仕事などの身近なトピックにおいて、文書の全体的な意味と目的を理解することができる。多くの場合、簡単な文と文法構造を理解でき、また時には限られた範囲であれば、複雑な文を理解できることもある。

19〜33点	このスコアレンジに該当する受験者は一般的に、よく使われる語彙と基本的な文法構造で書かれた、非常に短い文書内の身近な語句がわかる。身近なトピックに関する簡単な言葉を理解できることもある。一般的に、身近なトピックに関する非常に短い文書を理解することができる。特に、視覚的なヒントがあったりよく使われる形式で書かれたりしている、簡単なフレーズや文を理解できることもある。例えば、掲示物や予定表に書かれた詳細のいくつかを理解することができる。よく使われる語句を認識することで、簡単な文書の全体的な意味を理解できることもある。
15〜18点	このスコアレンジに該当する受験者は、非常に身近なニーズに関連する限られた語句がわかることがある。文脈に強く支えられた、非常によく使われる単語やフレーズを認識できる見込みがある。特にイラストなどのヒントが与えられた場合に「止まれ」「立ち入り禁止」などの簡単な指示について理解できる。時には1つのフレーズよりも長いものを理解できることもある。アルファベットの文字のみ認識できる受験者もいる可能性がある。

出典：

IIBC一般財団法人 国際ビジネスコミュニケーション協会

https://www.iibc-global.org/toeic/test/bridge_lr/guide04/guide04_02/score_descriptor.html#anchor01

TOEIC® Listening & Reading Testの形式について

　　TOEIC® L&R Testはリスニング（約45分間・100問）、リーディング（75分間・100問）、合計約2時間で200問に答えるマークシート方式の一斉客観テストです。出題形式は毎回同じで、解答はすべて問題用紙とは別の解答用紙に記入します。テストは英文のみで構成されており、英文和訳・和文英訳といった設問はありません。

テスト問題の構成

リスニング・セクション（約45分間・100問） **会話やナレーションを聞いて設問に解答します。**	
PART 1 （6問）	**写真描写問題（Photographs）** 1枚の写真について4つの短い説明文が1度だけ放送されます。説明文は印刷されていません。4つのうち、写真を最も的確に描写しているものを選び解答用紙にマークします。
PART 2 （25問）	**応答問題（Question-Response）** 1つの質問または文章とそれに対する3つの答えがそれぞれ1度だけ放送されます。印刷はされていません。設問に対して最もふさわしい答えを選び解答用紙にマークします。
PART 3 （39問）	**会話問題（Conversations）** 2人または3人の人物による会話が1度だけ放送されます。印刷はされていません。会話を聞いて問題用紙に印刷された設問（設問は放送される）と解答を読み、4つの答えの中から最も適当なものを選び解答用紙にマークします。会話の中で聞いたことと、問題用紙に印刷された図などで見た情報を関連づけて解答する設問もあります。各会話には設問が3問ずつあります。
PART 4 （30問）	**説明文問題（Talks）** アナウンスやナレーションのようなミニトークが1度だけ放送されます。印刷はされていません。各トークを聞いて問題用紙に印刷された設問（設問は放送される）と解答を読み、4つの答えの中から最も適当なものを選び解答用紙にマークします。トークの中で聞いたことと、問題用紙に印刷された図などで見た情報を関連づけて解答する設問もあります。各トークには質問が3問ずつあります。
リーディング・セクション（75分間・100問） **印刷された問題を読んで設問に解答します。**	
PART 5 （30問）	**短文穴埋め問題（Incomplete Sentences）** 不完全な文章を完成させるために、4つの答えの中から最も適当なものを選び解答用紙にマークします。

PART 6 （16問）	長文穴埋め問題（Text Completion） 不完全な文章を完成させるために、4つの答え（単語や句または一文）の中から最も適当なものを選び解答用紙にマークします。各長文には設問が4問ずつあります。
PART 7 （54問） 1つの文書：29問 複数の文書：25問	1つの文書、複数の文書（Single Passages / Multiple Passages） いろいろな文書が印刷されています。設問を読み、4つの答えの中から最も適当なものを選び解答用紙にマークします。文書内に新たな一文を挿入するのに最も適切な箇所を選ぶ設問もあります。各文書には設問が数問ずつあります。

TOEIC® L&R Testの結果について

Score Descriptor Table（レベル別評価の一覧表）

	リスニング・セクション
495 ～ 375点	一般的に以下の長所が認められます。 • 短い会話において、応答が間接的だったり、または簡単に予測できないようなものであっても、幅広い語彙（あまり使われない語彙、あるいは様々なトピックで用いられる語彙）を使用した話の主旨、目的、基本的な文脈が推測できる。 • 長い聴解文において、幅広く語彙が使用されていても、話の主旨、目的、基本的な文脈が推測できる。情報の繰り返しや言い換えがなかったり、広い範囲にわたって情報を関連付ける必要があるときでも、同じことができる。 • 短い会話において、否定構文が使用されていたり、構文が複雑だったり、難しい語彙が使われている場合でも詳細が理解できる。 • 長い聴解文において、広い範囲にわたって情報を関連付ける必要があったり、情報の繰り返しがなくても、話の詳細が理解できる。情報が言い換えられていたり、否定構文が使用されていても、詳細が理解できる。 　一般的に、このレベルのスコアを取得する受験者には、解答する際に、あまり使用されない文法や語彙が出てくるときにのみ、弱点が認められます。
370 ～ 275点	一般的に以下の長所が認められます。 • 短い会話において、特に語彙が難しくないときは、話の主旨、目的、基本的な文脈が推測できることもある。 • 長い聴解文において、情報の繰り返しや言い換えがあるときは、話の主旨、目的、基本的な文脈が理解できる。 • 短い会話において、簡単な、または中級レベルの語彙が使用されるときは、話の詳細が理解できる。 • 長い聴解文において、情報が繰り返され、解答に必要な情報が話の最初か最後に提示されるときは、話の詳細が理解できる。情報が少し言い換えられていても、詳細が理解できる。

370 〜 275点	一般的に以下の弱点が認められます。 • 短い会話において、応答が間接的だったり、簡単に予測できないとき、もしくは語彙が難しいときは、話の主旨、目的、基本的な文脈の理解が困難である。 • 長い聴解文において、広い範囲にわたって情報を関連付ける必要があるとき、もしくは難しい語彙が使用されるときは、話の主旨、目的、基本的な文脈が理解できない。 • 短い会話において、構文が複雑なときや、難しい語彙が使われている場合は、話の詳細が理解できない。否定構文が使用されるときは、詳細が理解できないことが多い。 • 長い聴解文において、広い範囲にわたって情報を関連付ける必要があるとき、もしくは情報が繰り返されないときは、話の詳細が理解できない。言い換えられた情報、または難しい文法的な構造はほとんど理解できない。
270 〜 5点	一般的に以下の長所が認められます。 • 写真描写において、写真の主旨に関する短い（一文の）記述が理解できる。 • 長い聴解文において、情報が何度も繰り返されたり、語彙が簡単なときは、話の主旨、目的、基本的な文脈が理解できることもある。 • 短い会話や写真描写において、語彙が簡単で、話のごく一部を理解すればよいときは、話の詳細や写真に関する記述が理解できる。 • 長い聴解文において、解答に必要な情報が話の最初か最後に提示され、問題中に使用されている表現と一致するときは、話の詳細が理解できる。 ※170点以下のスコアを取得した受験者には、200点前後のスコアを取得した受験者の長所がいくらか認められることがありますが、成績はより不安定になりがちです。 一般的に以下の弱点が認められます。 • 短い会話において、表現が直接的で、予想外の情報が提示されることがなくても、話の主旨、目的、基本的な文脈が理解できない。 • 長い聴解文において、広い範囲にわたって情報を関連付ける必要があるとき、もしくはやや難しい語彙が使用されるときは、話の主旨、目的、基本的な文脈が理解できない。 • 短い会話において、やや難しい語彙が使用されるとき、もしくは構文が複雑なときは、話の詳細が理解できない。否定構文が使用されるときは、詳細が理解できない。 • 長い聴解文において、解答に必要な情報が話の途中で提示されたときは、話の詳細が理解できない。言い換えられた情報や難しい文法的な構造が理解できない。

リーディング・セクション

420 ～ 325点	一般的に以下の長所が認められます。 ・文章の主旨や目的が推測できる。詳細が推測できる。 ・意味を読み取ることができる。言い換えがあっても、事実に基づく情報が理解できる。 ・章に使用されている語彙や文法が難しいときでも、文章の限られた範囲内では情報を関連付けることができる。 ・中級レベルの語彙が理解できる。文脈中の難しい語彙、よく使用される単語の例外的な意味、慣用句的な使い方が理解できることもある。 ・規則に基づいた文法構造が理解できる。また、難しく、複雑で、あまり使用されない文法的な構造が理解できる。 一般的に以下の弱点が認められます。 ・文章内の広い範囲にわたる情報を関連付けることができない。 ・難しい語彙、よく使用される単語の例外的な意味、または慣用句的な使い方が理解できないこともある。似たような意味で使われる複数の単語は、区別できないことが多い。
320 ～ 225点	一般的に以下の長所が認められます。 ・限られた長さの文章においては、簡単な推測ができる。 ・文章中に使われているのと同じ表現が問題に使用されているときは、事実に基づく情報に関する問題に正答できる。正しい選択肢が文章中の情報を簡単に言い換えたものであれば、事実に基づく情報に関する問題に答えられることもある。 ・一つの文、または二つの文にわたる情報を関連付けることができることもある。 ・簡単な語彙が理解できる。中級レベルの語彙を理解できることもある。 ・よく使用される、規則に基づいた文法構造が理解できる。文法以外に難しい言語的要素（難しい語彙が使われている、情報を関連付ける必要がある）がある場合でも、文法的に正しい選択肢が選べる。 一般的に以下の弱点が認められます。 ・言い換え、または情報の関連付けが必要な推測ができない。 ・事実に基づく情報を、難しい語彙を使用して言い換えた場合は、理解する能力は非常に限られている。解答するときは、問題に使用されているのと同じ単語や句を文章の中から探すことに頼ることが多い。 ・二つ以上の文にわたって情報を関連付けることができないことが多い。

320 〜 225点	• 難しい語彙、よく使用される単語の例外的な意味、または慣用句的な使い方が理解できない。似たような意味で使われる複数の単語は区別できないことが多い。 • より難しい、複雑な、またはあまり使用されない文法構造が理解できない。
220 〜 5点	一般的に以下の長所が認められます。 • あまり広い範囲を読む必要がないとき、ならびに文章中に使われているのと同じ表現が問題に使用されているときは、事実に基づく情報に関する問題に正答できる。 • 簡単な語彙、よく使用される句が理解できる。 • あまり広い範囲を読む必要がないときは、よく使用される、規則に基づいた文法構造が理解できる。 ※120点以下のスコアを取得した受験者には、150点前後のスコアを取得した受験者の長所がいくらか認められることがありますが、成績はより不安定になりがちです。 一般的に以下の弱点が認められます。 • 文章中の情報について、推測ができない。 • 事実に基づく情報の、言い換えが理解できない。解答するとき、問題に使用されているのと同じ単語や句を文章の中から探すことに頼る。 • 一つの文中の情報さえ、関連付けることができないことが多い。 • 限られた語彙しか理解できない。 • 文法以外に難しい言語的要素（難しい語彙が使用されている、情報を関連付ける必要がある）がある場合は、簡単な文法構造も理解できない。

出典：
IIBC 一般財団法人国際ビジネスコミュニケーション協会
https://www.iibc-global.org/toeic/test/lr/guide04/guide04_02/score_descriptor.html

TOEIC Bridge® Listening & Reading Tests と
TOEIC® Listening & Reading Test の比較

　以下の表は、一般財団法人　国際ビジネスコミュニケーション協会によって作成されました。日本と韓国の 15,569 名の受験者データを基に TOEIC Bridge® L&R Tests のスコアから、それに対応する TOEIC® L&R Test のスコアを予測したものです。

TOEIC Bridge® L&R Tests	90	100	110	120	130	140	150	160
TOEIC® L&R Test	230	260	280	310	345	395	470	570

出典：

IIBC 一般財団法人　国際ビジネスコミュニケーション協会

http://www.toeic.or.jp/library/toeic_data/bridge/pdf/data/Comparison_BridgeandTOEIC.pdf

TOEIC Bridge® Listening & Reading Tests と
TOEIC® Listening & Reading Test の申し込み方法

　TOEIC Bridge® L&R Tests および、TOEIC® L&R Test の公開テストを受験するには、IIBC 一般財団法人国際ビジネスコミュニケーション協会の公式ホームページからインターネットを通しての申し込みが必要です。詳しくは下記の公式ホームページをご覧ください。

TOEIC Bridge® L&R Tests

https://www.iibc-global.org/toeic/test/bridge_lr.html

TOEIC® L&R Test

https://www.iibc-global.org/toeic/test/lr/guide01.html

Contents

Crossing the TOEIC Bridge®

−New Edition−

Eating Out

🎧 **Listening Section**

👆 *Before Listening*

☑ **Vocabulary check**

Choose the correct meaning for each word or phrase.

1. co-worker	(	)	**2.** eat out	(	)
3. empty	(	)	**4.** order	(	)
5. make a reservation	(	)	**6.** serve	(	)

外食する	注文する	同僚
予約をする	給仕する、（食事等を）出す	空いている

🎧 **Part 1 Four Pictures**

You will see a set of four pictures, and you will hear one short phrase or sentence. Look at the set of pictures. Choose the picture that the phrase or sentence best describes.

1.

(A)

(B)

2.

(A)

(B)

(C)

(D)

(C)

(D)

Ⓐ Ⓑ Ⓒ Ⓓ

Ⓐ Ⓑ Ⓒ Ⓓ

Part 2 Question-Response

You will hear some questions or statements. After each question or statement, you will hear and read four responses. Choose the best response to each question or statement.

3. (A) From 7:00 a.m. to 9:00 a.m.
   (B) It's my first time.
   (C) Bacon and eggs.
   (D) It starts at 7 p.m.   Ⓐ Ⓑ Ⓒ Ⓓ

4. (A) I like spaghetti.
   (B) No, I didn't have lunch.
   (C) Tomorrow at 7:00.
   (D) Sorry. I have to do my assignment.   Ⓐ Ⓑ Ⓒ Ⓓ

Part 3 Conversation

You will hear a short conversation. You will hear and read two questions about the conversation. Each question has four answer choices. Choose the best answer to each question.

5. Where does this conversation take place?
   (A) At a restaurant
   (B) At work
   (C) At home
   (D) At school   Ⓐ Ⓑ Ⓒ Ⓓ

6. What does the man suggest to the woman?
   (A) To eat out
   (B) To go home
   (C) To work late
   (D) To work out   Ⓐ Ⓑ Ⓒ Ⓓ

You will hear a short talk. You will hear and read two questions about the talk. Each question has four answer choices. Choose the best answer to each question.

7. **Why does the speaker make this announcement?**
   (A) To invite someone to a dinner party
   (B) To advertise a new restaurant chain
   (C) To cancel a reservation
   (D) To remind a co-worker of his schedule   Ⓐ Ⓑ Ⓒ Ⓓ

8. **What does the speaker ask listeners to do?**
   (A) Eat at home
   (B) Order a pizza to go
   (C) Call the speaker back
   (D) Make a reservation   Ⓐ Ⓑ Ⓒ Ⓓ

📖 Reading Section

🖋 *Before Reading*

☑ Vocabulary check

Choose the correct meaning for each word or phrase.

1. benefit   (   )   2. free repair service (   )
3. marketing   (   )   4. supervisor   (   )
5. financial condition (   )   6. pension   (   )

無料修理サービス	給付金	市場
財政状況	監督者	年金

4

Grammar

■ **be動詞** ■

be動詞は日本語の「～です」「～がいます（あります）」にあたり、主語の直後に置かれます。

（例） Mr. Hoffman **is** an accountant.（ホフマン氏は会計士です。）

He **was** in the Northern California branch.（彼は北カリフォルニア支店にいました。）

The documents **are** on the desk.（その書類は机の上にあります。）

be動詞には、以下の表に示されるように、am, is, are, was, were の5種類があり、主語や時制によって使い分けます。

		現在形（…は ～です。）	過去形（…は～でした。）
単数	私は	I am ～.	I was ～.
	あなたは	You are ～.	You were ～.
	彼は	He is ～.	He was ～.
	彼女は	She is ～.	She was ～.
	それは	It is ～.	It was ～.
複数	私たちは	We are ～.	We were ～.
	あなたたちは	You are ～.	You were ～.
	彼らは 彼女らは それらは	They are ～.	They were ～.

否定文を作る時は、be動詞の後にnotを入れます。

例えば、Mr. Hoffman is **not** an accountant.（ホフマン氏は会計士ではありません）のようになります。

疑問文を作る時は、主語とbe動詞の語順を逆にします。

すなわち、Is Mr. Hoffman an accountant?（ホフマン氏は会計士ですか）のようになります。

（例題） My uncle _____ a sales manager at ABC Corporation last year.

(A) is　　　(B) was　　　(C) are　　　(D) were

（解答） (B) was（私の叔父は昨年ABC会社の販売部長でした。）

この文の最後に書かれている last year に注目すると、過去のことを表す文章であることがわかります。よって、My uncle を代名詞に置き換えると He になるので、be動詞は過去形の was を選ばなければなりません。

Choose the correct word to complete each sentence.

(1) Mr. Lee and Ms. Wong _____ the supervisors of this factory.
  (A) is   (B) are   Ⓐ Ⓑ

(2) The financial condition of the company _____ not good two years ago.
  (A) is   (B) was   Ⓐ Ⓑ

Part **1** Sentence Completion

You will read some sentences. Each one has a space where a word or phrase is missing. Choose the best answer to complete the sentence.

9. Customer service managers _____ all busy doing the marketing research last night.
  (A) is
  (B) are
  (C) was
  (D) were   Ⓐ Ⓑ Ⓒ Ⓓ

10. Pensions _____ the most important benefit.
  (A) is
  (B) are
  (C) be
  (D) has   Ⓐ Ⓑ Ⓒ Ⓓ

11. Our company's policy _____ to offer free repair service.
  (A) are
  (B) is
  (C) were
  (D) be   Ⓐ Ⓑ Ⓒ Ⓓ

12. We were studying law at university, and both of us _____ lawyers now.
  (A) are
  (B) were
  (C) is
  (D) be   Ⓐ Ⓑ Ⓒ Ⓓ

You will read a short text. Each one has three spaces where a word, phrase, or sentence is missing. For each space, choose the best answer to complete the text.

Renovation of BBQ Garden

We are sorry but — **(13)** — restaurant is closed for kitchen renovation from December 17 to 23. We will reopen — **(14)** — December 24. — **(15)** —.

---

13. (A) us
(B) our
(C) them
(D) their

(A) (B) (C) (D)

14. (A) on
(B) in
(C) at
(D) to

(A) (B) (C) (D)

15. (A) Why don't you go out for dinner with us?
(B) Thank you for your understanding.
(C) Enjoy the rest of the day.
(D) See you tomorrow.

(A) (B) (C) (D)

You will read a text. Choose the best answer to each question.

Questions 16 - 18 refer to the following notice.

LINDEN COURT RESTAURANT

Monday thru Saturday

Lunch: 11:30 a.m. – 3:30 p.m.

Dinner: 5:30 p.m. – 9:00 p.m.

Sunday

Brunch: 8:00 a.m. – 1:00 p.m.

Dinner: 4:00 p.m. – 7:00 p.m.

We serve the daily dinner special for just $11.95, and the Sunday dinner special for $15.75!

---

16. **When does dinner start on Tuesday?**
    (A) At 3:30 p.m.
    (B) At 4:00 p.m.
    (C) At 5:30 p.m.
    (D) At 7:00 p.m.   Ⓐ Ⓑ Ⓒ Ⓓ

17. **How much is the Sunday special?**
    (A) $7.00
    (B) $11.95
    (C) $15.75
    (D) Not mentioned   Ⓐ Ⓑ Ⓒ Ⓓ

18. **When can people NOT have lunch?**
    (A) Monday at noon
    (B) Wednesday at 1:00 p.m.
    (C) Sunday at 4:00 p.m.
    (D) Every day at 12:30 p.m.   Ⓐ Ⓑ Ⓒ Ⓓ

column

TOEIC Bridge® L&R TestsからTOEIC® L&R Testへ（対策編）

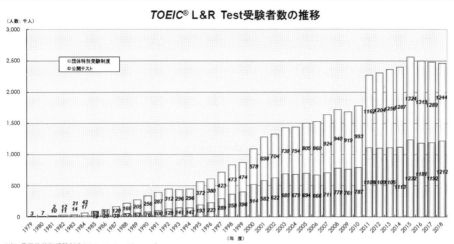

TOEIC® L&R Test受験者数の推移

(注) ①団体特別受験制度（IP: Institutional Program）
　　　・・・企業・大学などの団体が、所属社員・学生などを対象に随時実施する受験制度
　　　②公開テスト
　　　・・・当協会の管理下で実施し、個人が直接申し込みをする受験制度　　　資料提供元: 一般財団法人 国際ビジネスコミュニケーション協会

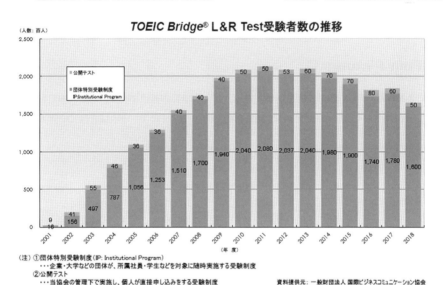

TOEIC Bridge® L&R Test受験者数の推移

(注) ①団体特別受験制度（IP: Institutional Program）
　　　・・・企業・大学などの団体が、所属社員・学生などを対象に随時実施する受験制度
　　　②公開テスト
　　　・・・当協会の管理下で実施し、個人が直接申し込みをする受験制度　　　資料提供元: 一般財団法人 国際ビジネスコミュニケーション協会

　グラフから、TOEIC® L&R TestとTOEIC Bridge® L&R Tests が英語力を測るテストとして広く活用されていることがわかります。TOEIC Bridge® L&R Tests の出題形式は、TOEIC® L&R Testに類似しています。初級レベルの学習者は、TOEIC Bridge® L&R Testsの対策をしながら英語学習を進めることによって、将来的にはTOEIC® L&R Test受験へとスムーズに移行することができます。

　IIBC一般財団法人国際ビジネスコミュニケーション協会のホームページでは、TOEIC Bridge® L&R Testsは、TOEIC® L&R Testより、日常的で身近な話題が取り上げられ、リスニング問題のスピードもゆっくりだと公表されています。ほぼすべての語彙や表現が高校卒業時までに既習のものなので、大学生がTOEIC Bridge® L&R Testsを受験する場合、知らない単語を目にすることはほとんどないということになります。そのため、TOEIC® L&R Testでのスコアに伸び悩んでいる学習者は、先にTOEIC Bridge® L&R Testsの対策をし、7割以上正解できるようになってから、TOEIC Bridge® L&R Testsに挑戦するとよいでしょう。

2 Travel

 ## Listening Section

♠ *Before Listening*

☑ Vocabulary check

Choose the correct meaning for each word or phrase.

1. aisle seat ( ) 2. delay ( )
3. due to ( ) 4. passenger ( )
5. round-trip ( ) 6. timetable ( )

乗客	遅らせる	〜が原因で
往復の	時刻表	通路側の席

6 Part **1** Four Pictures

You will see a set of four pictures, and you will hear one short phrase or sentence. Look at the set of pictures. Choose the picture that the phrase or sentence best describes.

1.

(A) (B)

(C) (D)

Ⓐ Ⓑ Ⓒ Ⓓ

2.

(A) (B)

(C) (D)

Ⓐ Ⓑ Ⓒ Ⓓ

Part 2 Question-Response

You will hear some questions or statements. After each question or statement, you will hear and read four responses. Choose the best response to each question or statement.

3. (A) Flight 421.
   (B) A round-trip ticket, please.
   (C) Aisle seat, please.
   (D) I would prefer meat. Ⓐ Ⓑ Ⓒ Ⓓ

4. (A) Next weekend.
   (B) Last Saturday.
   (C) Yes, he is new in town.
   (D) I came back last night. Ⓐ Ⓑ Ⓒ Ⓓ

Part 3 Conversation

You will hear a short conversation. You will hear and read two questions about the conversation. Each question has four answer choices. Choose the best answer to each question.

5. **Where are the speakers?**
   (A) At a train station
   (B) At a bus terminal
   (C) At an airport
   (D) At a travel agency Ⓐ Ⓑ Ⓒ Ⓓ

6. **What will the man probably do next?**
   (A) Double-check the timetable
   (B) Check the phone number
   (C) Contact the travel agency
   (D) Go back to the hotel Ⓐ Ⓑ Ⓒ Ⓓ

Part 4 Talk

You will hear a short talk. You will hear and read two questions about each talk. The question has four answer choices. Choose the best answer to each question.

7. **Where does this conversation take place?**
   (A) At a train station
   (B) At an airport
   (C) At a ferry terminal
   (D) At a bus terminal

8. **Why is the flight delayed?**
   (A) Due to a mechanical problem
   (B) Due to the pilot's health problem
   (C) Due to a workers' strike
   (D) Due to bad weather   (A) (B) (C) (D)

Reading Section

♠ *Before Reading*

☑ Vocabulary check

Choose the correct meaning for each word or phrase.

1. available	(	)	2. charge	(	)
3. tax	(	)	4. cost reduction	(	)
5. vice president	(	)	6. product	(	)

利用可能な	税金	副社長
料金	経費削減	製品

■ 一般動詞 ■

一般動詞は主語の直後に置き、動作や状態を表します。

動作	study（勉強する）、speak（話す）、meet（会う）
状態	know（知っている）、like（好む）、want（欲しい）

●3単元のsのつけ方

肯定文で主語がHe, She, It の時だけ-sがつきます。

		規則動詞（歩く）		不規則動詞（書く）	
		現在形	過去形	現在形	過去形
単数	I You	walk	walked	write	wrote
	He She It	walks		writes	
複数	We You They	walk		write	

●疑問文・否定文の作り方

疑問文

	You	meet ⇓ meet	your client.
Do	you		your client?
	He	meets ⇓ meet	his client.
Does	he		his client?

疑問文：主語がI, You, We, Theyのときは Doを、He, She, Itの時は Doesを、過去形の場合はDid を文頭に置き、動詞は原形（-s のつかない形）にします。

否定文

You		meet ⇓ meet	your client.
You	don't		your client.
He		meets ⇓ meet	his client.
He	doesn't		his client.

否定文：主語の後ろにdon't, doesn't を、過去形の場合はdidn'tを 置き、動詞は原形にします。

●過去形

過去形は規則動詞の場合 -ed がつきますが、不規則動詞は動詞の形そのものが変わる ので、すべて覚えておかなければなりません。不規則動詞の一覧表は巻末(pp.128-129) にありますので、そちらを参照してください。

Choose the correct word to complete each sentence

(1) Richard didn't _____ about his work experience at the interview.
(A) talked   (B) talk   Ⓐ Ⓑ

(2) Your presentation always _____ the audience.
(A) attract   (B) attracts   Ⓐ Ⓑ

Part 1 Sentence Completion

You will read some sentences. Each one has a space where a word or phrase is missing. Choose the best answer to complete the sentence.

9. The vice president's speech _____ for 30 minutes.
(A) lasts
(B) lasting
(C) last
(D) be lasting   Ⓐ Ⓑ Ⓒ Ⓓ

10. Do they _____ information about their new product?
(A) provide
(B) providing
(C) provides
(D) provision   Ⓐ Ⓑ Ⓒ Ⓓ

11. Last year, the company _____ that it would achieve remarkable cost reductions.
(A) announces
(B) announced
(C) announcement
(D) announcing   Ⓐ Ⓑ Ⓒ Ⓓ

12. According to Mr. Henry, Dell Electronics _____ financially this year.
(A) struggle
(B) are struggle
(C) is struggling
(D) were struggled   Ⓐ Ⓑ Ⓒ Ⓓ

You will read a short text. Each one has three spaces where a word, phrase, or sentence is missing. For each space, choose the best answer to complete the text.

Dear Ben,

Thank you very much for your — (**13**) —. I am sorry but the day trip to Stonehenge is already full. — (**14**) —, the half-day city tour is still available. — (**15**) —. Thanks.

Molly Brown

Desmond Tours Ltd.

---

13. (A) order
 (B) help
 (C) inquiry
 (D) advice   Ⓐ Ⓑ Ⓒ Ⓓ

14. (A) Also
 (B) Hence
 (C) Although
 (D) However   Ⓐ Ⓑ Ⓒ Ⓓ

15. (A) Please let me know what you want to do.
 (B) To Stonehenge, it will take more than six hours by bus.
 (C) I've got your order.
 (D) Did you have a wonderful time?   Ⓐ Ⓑ Ⓒ Ⓓ

You will read a text. Choose the best answer to each question.

Questions 16 - 18 refer to the following receipt.

Bartlesville Hotel
2202 North Highway 35
Bartlesville, OK 74003
918-577-9999

Customer name: PATEL, Sanjay

Room: 1 Single
Daily rate: $79.00 + tax
Nights: 1
Guests: 1
Charges:

Dates	Room	Phone	Tax	Total
1/5	$79	0	$10.27	$89.27
TOTAL:	$79		$10.27	$89.27

THANK YOU. PLEASE VISIT US AGAIN!

We hope you have enjoyed your stay. Please call us toll-free to make reservations for your next stay:

Tel. 0200-353-2481

16. **What was the total charge for Mr. Patel's room?**
    (A) $10.27   (B) $79
    (C) $89.27   (D) $90   Ⓐ Ⓑ Ⓒ Ⓓ

17. **How long did Mr. Patel stay at the hotel?**
    (A) One night   (B) Five days
    (C) One week   (D) One month   Ⓐ Ⓑ Ⓒ Ⓓ

18. **How can Mr. Patel make a next reservation?**
    (A) By visiting the website   (B) By e-mailing
    (C) By faxing   (D) By calling   Ⓐ Ⓑ Ⓒ Ⓓ

column

TOEIC® L&R Test（リスニング編1）

　初めてTOEIC® L&R Testの学習をする人の中には、いくらリスニング・セクションの問題を解いても、なかなか正解できず、がっかりして、途中で学習を断念する人がいます。その人たちが正解できなかった原因を調べてみると、意外にも単に中学1年生レベルの英単語が聞き取れていなかっただけということがよくあります。英語の綴りを見ればすぐにその意味が理解できるのに、音声になった瞬間、その意味がわからなくなるという経験はありませんか。音声を聞いて、瞬時にその意味が理解できるようになるためには、ディクテーション練習が効果的です。ディクテーションとは、英文を聞いて、その英文を書き取るという練習方法ですが、以下のような3ステップで行うと非常に効果的です。

1. まずは文単位で聞こえた英文を書き取る

　ディクテーション練習をする際には、英文を1文聞いてから音声を止め、聞こえた音声を紙に書き取ります。聞き取れない部分があれば、再度、文全体を聞き直すようにしてください。どうしても英語の綴りが思い浮かばない場合は、カタカナでもかまいませんので、聞こえた音をメモしておきます。

2. 前後関係から聞き取れなかった単語を推測する

　次に聞き取れなかった単語を推測します。前後関係から、どのような単語が入りそうか、品詞は何かなどを推測してください。この時に文法の知識が役立ちます。例えば、現在進行形の文章であれば be 動詞の後に –ing 形が続くはずなのに、書き取った英文では –ing が抜けている場合、自分がこの音を聞き落したこと、そして、この音が思っているよりも小さく読まれていることに気づくでしょう。

3. スクリプトを使って、文字を見ながら音声と意味を再確認する

　書き取った単語が間違っていたら、色ペンで正しい単語をその横に書いておくとよいでしょう。どのような単語を自分が聞き間違えたのか、または聞き取れなかったのかをきちんと把握しておけば同じミスを防ぐことができます。同時に知らなかった単語の意味も確認しておきましょう。

　以上のような3ステップで、繰り返しディクテーション練習をすれば、徐々に英語の音を理解し、その特徴をつかめるようになります。そして読まれた英文の意味も徐々にわかるようになっていきます。

3 Amusement

 ## Listening Section

🖐 *Before Listening*

☑ Vocabulary check

Choose the correct meaning for each word or phrase.

1. apologize   (   )   **2.** attraction   (   )

3. join   (   )   **4.** remodel   (   )

5. ride   (   )   **6.** be sold out   (   )

改装する	参加する	乗る
売り切れになる	謝罪する	呼び物

🎧10 Part 1 Four Pictures

You will see a set of four pictures, and you will hear one short phrase or sentence. Look at the set of pictures. Choose the picture that the phrase or sentence best describes.

1.

(A)   (B)

2.

(A)   (B)

(C)   (D)

(C)   (D)

 Ⓐ Ⓑ Ⓒ Ⓓ   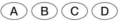 Ⓐ Ⓑ Ⓒ Ⓓ

Part 2 Question-Response

You will hear some questions or statements. After each question or statement, you will hear and read four responses. Choose the best response to each question or statement.

3. (A) It starts at 8:00.
   (B) It's at my house.
   (C) He is on the way.
   (D) No, she doesn't feel well.

4. (A) It's the band's final concert tour.
   (B) On Friday at 7:30.
   (C) Yes, I need three tickets.
   (D) At the Civic Center.

 Part 3 Conversation

You will hear a short conversation. You will hear and read two questions about the conversation. Each question has four answer choices. Choose the best answer to each question.

5. **What are the speakers discussing?**
   (A) Menus for dinner
   (B) Movies to see
   (C) Plans for tonight
   (D) Places to visit

6. **What will the woman probably do next?**
   (A) Tell her friends' names
   (B) Tell the man where and when to get together
   (C) Ask the man to join the dinner
   (D) Go to the movies with the man

You will hear a short talk. You will hear and read two questions about each talk. The question has four answer choices. Choose the best answer to each question.

7. **What does the speaker say about Surabaya Zoo?**
   (A) The zoo is closed all day.
   (B) Lions and tigers can be seen all day.
   (C) Tickets are all sold out.
   (D) Giraffes can be viewed.   Ⓐ Ⓑ Ⓒ Ⓓ

8. **Look at the schedule. What time does the giraffe show probably start?**
   (A) 11:50
   (B) 13:00
   (C) 13:30
   (D) 16:30   Ⓐ Ⓑ Ⓒ Ⓓ

Today's schedule

Penguin aquarium	10:45-11:50
Monkey circus	13:00-13:25
Rhino petting	16:00-16:25

📖 Reading Section

✋ *Before Reading*

☑ Vocabulary check

Choose the correct meaning for each word or phrase.

1. driver's license ( )   2. public transportation ( )
3. shipping cost ( )   4. valid ( )
5. viewer ( )   6. weight ( )

| 配送料 | 公共交通機関 | 有効な |
| 視聴者 | 重さ | 運転免許証 |

■ 品詞 ■

英語の品詞には次のようなものがあります。

● 名　詞：物の名前や物質、抽象的なものを表します。（例：pen, water, love）

● 代名詞：名詞の代わりに使われます。（例：My mother sometimes makes cakes. I like them (cakes) very much.）

● 動　詞：動作や状態を表します。（例：I'll write a letter to you.）

● 形容詞：名詞を修飾します。（例：a beautiful woman）

● 副　詞：動詞や形容詞、または文全体を修飾し、語尾に -ly がつくものが多いです。

　　　　　• They decorate the room beautifully.

　　　　　（下線部の beautifully「美しく」は、decorate という動詞を修飾しています。）

　　　　　• It is awfully cold today.

　　　　　（下線部の awfully「猛烈に」は、cold という形容詞を修飾しています。）

　　　　　• Unfortunately, I missed the last train.

　　　　　（下線部の Unfortunately「不運にも」は、I missed the last train という文全体を修飾しています。）

● 前置詞：主に名詞や代名詞の前で用いられ、in, on, at, with, of などがあります。

　　　　　（例：There is a book on the desk.　I had a meeting with them.）

● 接続詞：語と語、句と句、節と節を結びつけるために用いられ、and, but, or, so などがあります。

　　　　　（例：He speaks English and French.　I was tired, but I worked overtime.）

● 間投詞：驚きや、怒り、喜びの感情を表します。（例：Oh!　Wow!）

品詞は以下のようなことに注意すると見分けやすくなります。

品詞	特徴	例	
名詞	-ment, -tion, -ness, -ce 等で終わる語	encouragement（励まし） communication（連絡） happiness（幸福） presence（出席）	agreement（同意） vacation（休暇） kindness（優しさ） absence（欠席）
形容詞	-able, -ful, -tive 等で終わる語	capable（能力がある） beautiful（美しい） attractive（魅力的な）	probable（起こりそうな） awful（猛烈な） creative（創造力のある）
副詞	-ly で終わる語	attractively（魅力的に）	awfully（猛烈に）

Choose the correct word to complete each sentence.

(1) Shipping cost is _____ related to the weight of the package.
   (A) directions   (B) directly   Ⓐ Ⓑ

(2) The company _____ a strong team for the project.
   (A) requires   (B) requirement   Ⓐ Ⓑ

Part ❶ Sentence Completion
_____

You will read some sentences. Each one has a space where a word or phrase is missing. Choose the best answer to complete the sentence.

9. Computer World _____ some products for small and medium-sized businesses.
   (A) introduce
   (B) introduced
   (C) introduction
   (D) introducing   Ⓐ Ⓑ Ⓒ Ⓓ

10. San Antonia Hotel is _____ by public transportation.
   (A) accessibility
   (B) access
   (C) accessible
   (D) accessibly   Ⓐ Ⓑ Ⓒ Ⓓ

11. It is difficult to get a seat without a _____.
   (A) reservation
   (B) reserve
   (C) reservations
   (D) reserved   Ⓐ Ⓑ Ⓒ Ⓓ

12. You must show a _____ driver's license or an ID.
   (A) validity
   (B) validation
   (C) valid
   (D) validly   Ⓐ Ⓑ Ⓒ Ⓓ

Part 2 Text Completion

You will read a short text. Each one has three spaces where a word, phrase, or sentence is missing. For each space, choose the best answer to complete the text.

Dear visitors,

*Welcome to the Teddy Bear Museum. We — (**13**) — various kinds of teddy bears from around the world.*

*Today's museum tour starts from 10:30. — (**14**) —. You can also enjoy — (**15**) — at our museum shop. We are open until 4:30 p.m. Have a good day.*

13. (A) exhibition
    (B) exhibit
    (C) explore
    (D) exploring
    Ⓐ Ⓑ Ⓒ Ⓓ

14. (A) It's free.
    (B) That's all for today.
    (C) It was fun.
    (D) They are full.
    Ⓐ Ⓑ Ⓒ Ⓓ

15. (A) purchase
    (B) buying
    (C) shopping
    (D) stores
    Ⓐ Ⓑ Ⓒ Ⓓ

You will read a text. Choose the best answer to each question.

Questions 16 - 18 refer to the following schedule.

COTV
Your Local Community Television Station
Afternoon / Evening Schedule*

Monday to Friday		Saturday & Sunday	
12:00 - 3:00	*The Afternoon Show*	12:00 - 3:00	*Local News and Events*
3:00 - 4:00	*Around Town*	3:00 - 4:00	*Kids' Story Hour*
4:00 - 6:00	*Sports Talk*	4:00 - 6:00	*Weekend Concert*
6:00 - 7:00	*News of the Day*	6:00 - 7:00	*News of the Day*
7:00 - 9:00	*Night Out*	7:00 - 9:00	*World Music Tour*

To see any of our shows repeated on our website, go to www.cotvshows.com. For other information, call us at 409-3487.

16. **When is probably a good time for children to watch COTV?**
    (A) Saturday 3:00 to 4:00
    (B) Monday 6:00 to 7:00
    (C) Wednesday 3:00 to 4:00
    (D) Saturday 4:00 to 5:00

17. **When is probably a good time for viewers interested in music?**
    (A) Monday 4:00 to 6:00
    (B) Tuesday 7:00 to 9:00
    (C) Saturday 7:00 to 9:00
    (D) Sunday 6:00 to 7:00

18. **What do the viewers have to do to see a show again?**
    (A) Call at 409-3487
    (B) Go to the TV station
    (C) Turn on the TV
    (D) Visit the COTV website

column

TOEIC® L&R Test（リスニング編 2）

　TOEIC Bridge® L&R TestsとTOEIC® L&R Testの学習を始めたばかりの学習者にとっては、リスニング・セクションは非常に難しく、何を言っているのかほとんど聞き取れないという声をしばしば耳にします。

　では、どうすれば、ほとんど聞き取れないという状態から、主題と要点くらいは聞き取れるという状態へとレベルアップできるのでしょうか。

1．繰り返しリスニング

　「一度聞いて終わり」ではなく、音声を繰り返し聞いてください。何度も聞いているうちに少しずつ聞き取れる部分が増えていきます。音声を何度聞いてもわからないときは、音声を文字に起こした「スクリプト」を活用してください。

2．英文内容を理解

　スクリプトを見ながら、知らなかった単語を調べ、英文の内容や訳を確認し、理解するようにしてください。

3．スクリプトを見ながらリスニング

　次に、スクリプトを見ながら音声を聞いて、「今読まれている箇所は、ここだな」と確認してください。

4．スクリプトを見ながらシャドーイング

　再度音声を流し、スクリプトを見ながら読まれている箇所を声に出して言うようにします。英語が流れた直後に、それを追いかけるようにして声に出して読んでいくという方法で練習しますが、これをシャドーイングと呼んでいます。何度も繰り返しシャドーイング練習することで、英文のナチュラル・スピードに徐々に慣れてきます。

5．スクリプトを見ないでシャドーイング

　2、3回シャドーイング練習をして、英文のスピードに慣れてきたら、次はスクリプトをまったく見ない状態、すなわち英語の文字に頼らない状態でシャドーイングをしてみましょう。語彙や文章の意味を完全に理解した状態で、文字を見ずにシャドーイングができるように心がけましょう。

　リスニング問題を解いた後に正答を確認し、解答して終わりにするのではなく、間違った問題は、スクリプトを利用してこのような練習をしてください。そうすることで徐々に英語の音が聞き取れるようになっていきます。そして最終的にはテストでのスコアアップにもつながります。

4 Meetings

 Listening Section

☝ *Before Listening*

☑ Vocabulary check

Choose the correct meaning for each word or phrase.

1. attend   (   )   2. order   (   )

3. organizing committee (   )   4. postpone (   )

5. reschedule   (   )   6. subject   (   )

組織委員会	議題	出席する
順番	（予定などを）再調整する	延期する

🎧14 Part 1 Four Pictures

You will see a set of four pictures, and you will hear one short phrase or sentence. Look at the set of pictures. Choose the picture that the phrase or sentence best describes.

1.
(A)   (B)
(C)   (D)

Ⓐ Ⓑ Ⓒ Ⓓ

2.
(A)   (B)
(C)   (D)

Ⓐ Ⓑ Ⓒ Ⓓ

You will hear some questions or statements. After each question or statement, you will hear and read four responses. Choose the best response to each question or statement.

3. (A) It's about the new marketing campaign.
   (B) At 4:00 on Thursday.
   (C) It's a monthly meeting.
   (D) In room 2373.
   Ⓐ Ⓑ Ⓒ Ⓓ

4. (A) Ten people will attend.
   (B) It's in the room.
   (C) Yes, it did.
   (D) I don't know.
   Ⓐ Ⓑ Ⓒ Ⓓ

🎧16 **Part 3** **Conversation**

You will hear a short conversation. You will hear and read two questions about the conversation. Each question has four answer choices. Choose the best answer to each question.

5. **What is the conversation about?**
   (A) A schedule change
   (B) Road conditions
   (C) A talk about politics
   (D) A traffic accident
   Ⓐ Ⓑ Ⓒ Ⓓ

6. **Look at the chart. When will the man probably arrive?**
   (A) Just before 9:00
   (B) Just before 10:30
   (C) After the lunch break
   (D) After 15:25
   Ⓐ Ⓑ Ⓒ Ⓓ

Time	Guest speakers	Title
9:00-10:25	Andrew Mollison	Favorable Business Manners
10:30-11:55	Kenny Johnson	Our Marketing Strategy
Lunch break		
13:30-15:25	Molly Sanchez	The Role of Future Managers

Part 4 Talk

You will hear a short talk. You will hear and read two questions about each talk. The question has four answer choices. Choose the best answer to each question.

7. **What does the man want the woman to do?**
   (A) Change the date for the meeting
   (B) Attend the meeting for him
   (C) Take the man to the hospital
   (D) Apologize for the woman's mistake   Ⓐ Ⓑ Ⓒ Ⓓ

8. **When does the man go back to work?**
   (A) This afternoon
   (B) Tomorrow
   (C) Next week
   (D) Sometime this week   Ⓐ Ⓑ Ⓒ Ⓓ

Reading Section

♠ *Before Reading*

☑ Vocabulary check

Choose the correct meaning for each word or phrase.

1. agreement	(	)	2. book	(	)
3. budget	(	)	4. contact	(	)
5. quarter	(	)	6. sales figures	(	)

合意	予算	予約する
連絡を取る	売上高	四半期

■ 自動詞・他動詞 ■

自動詞と他動詞の違い

●自動詞「動詞の直後に目的語（名詞）を必要としない」

- Oil prices rise sharply.（石油価格が急に上がっています。）
          自動詞

自動詞は目的語がなくても文の意味が成り立ちます。Oil prices rise.（石油価格が上がっています）だけでも十分意味が通じます。動詞の後ろに置かれている sharply（急に）は名詞ではないので目的語ではありません。

●他動詞「動詞の直後に目的語（名詞）を必要とする」

- Rachel raises three little kids.（レイチェルは3人の小さな子供を育てています。）
          他動詞   目的語

他動詞は目的語がないと文の意味が成り立ちません。three little kidsという目的語がないと、「何を」育てているのかわからなくなります。

●自動詞と他動詞の区別がつきにくいため注意が必要な語（綴りが似ている）

現在形	過去形	過去分詞形	意味	
rise	rose	risen	上がる	自動詞
raise	raised	raised	上げる	他動詞
lie	lay	lain	横たわる	自動詞
lay	laid	laid	横たえる	他動詞

●自動詞と間違えやすいため注意が必要な他動詞

marry（結婚する）	enter（入る）	discuss（議論する）
approach（近づく）	mention（述べる）	attend（出席する）
reach（達する）	resemble（似ている）	

これらは他動詞なので、動詞の直後に目的語となる名詞を置かなければなりませんが、discuss about the problem（その問題について話し合う）や、marry with him（彼と結婚する）のように前置詞をはさんでしまいやすいので注意してください。about や with は不要です。

Choose the correct word to complete each sentence.

(1) Employees cannot _____ the building without their ID cards.
   (A) enter   (B) enter to   Ⓐ Ⓑ

(2) The problem _____ in the company's budget plan.
   (A) lays   (B) lies   Ⓐ Ⓑ

Part 1 Sentence Completion

You will read some sentences. Each one has a space where a word or phrase is missing. Choose the best answer to complete the sentence.

9. We finally _____ an agreement.
   (A) reached
   (B) reached to
   (C) reaching
   (D) reached with   Ⓐ Ⓑ Ⓒ Ⓓ

10. Our sales figures _____ by 25% last quarter.
   (A) raise
   (B) rise
   (C) raised
   (D) rose   Ⓐ Ⓑ Ⓒ Ⓓ

11. They _____ BioCera Inc. to meet their executives.
   (A) visited
   (B) visited to
   (C) are visited
   (D) visits   Ⓐ Ⓑ Ⓒ Ⓓ

12. If you have any questions, please _____ me at (805) 243-7518.
   (A) contacting
   (B) contact
   (C) contact to
   (D) contact with   Ⓐ Ⓑ Ⓒ Ⓓ

You will read a short text. Each one has three spaces where a word, phrase, or sentence is missing. For each space, choose the best answer to complete the text.

TO: Kristine Campbell <kris_camp1005@orange.com>
RE: Schedule Change

Dear Kristine,

Hello. — **(13)** — you hear about the schedule change? Today's meeting has — **(14)** —. We'll have a meeting tomorrow instead. — **(15)** —. Thanks.

Justin Bray
Sales manager

---

13. (A) Are
    (B) Were
    (C) Have
    (D) Did

    Ⓐ Ⓑ Ⓒ Ⓓ

14. (A) been cancelled
    (B) been cancelling
    (C) cancelled
    (D) become cancel

    Ⓐ Ⓑ Ⓒ Ⓓ

15. (A) You can take a day off tomorrow.
    (B) See you next week.
    (C) I hope you can make it.
    (D) They haven't set the date yet.

    Ⓐ Ⓑ Ⓒ Ⓓ

You will read a text. Choose the best answer to each question.

Question 16 - 18 refer to the following text message.

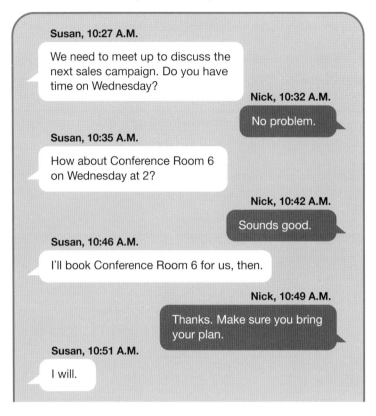

16. **Why will they get together?**
    (A) To talk about sales promotions
    (B) To clean the conference room
    (C) To book room 6
    (D) To prepare for the next meeting

17. **At 10:42 A.M., what does Nick likely mean when he writes, "Sounds good"?**
    (A) He wants to see Susan later.
    (B) He often uses that conference room.
    (C) He is available on Wednesday at 2:00.
    (D) He wants Susan to bring along her plan.

18. **What will Susan most likely do next?**
    (A) Make plans for lunch
    (B) Give a PowerPoint presentation
    (C) Cancel the meeting
    (D) Reserve the room

TOEIC® L&R Test学習法（文法 & 語彙編）

　文法や語彙の知識が豊富であればあるほど、問題が解きやすくなり、スコアアップにもつながることは言うまでもありません。それでは文法や語彙の知識を深めるために、どのような学習をすればよいのでしょうか。

1．高校生用の文法書を活用する

　TOEIC Bridge® L&R Test だけでなく、意外にも、TOEIC® L&R Testの文法問題もまた、高校までの既習範囲で構成されており、品詞や動詞の形に関する問題が多く出題される傾向にあります。

　文法に自信がない人は、単元別になっている高校の文法書を一通り読み、ルールを理解した上でTOEIC® L&R Testの問題をこなしていくと、より理解が深まり、効率的です。

　TOEIC® L&R Testの問題を解くときには、なぜその選択肢が正解なのか、その理由を自分の言葉で説明できるようにしておきましょう。説明できるということは、その文法が理解できているということを意味します。

　文法書は一読したらそれでおしまい、というわけではなく、文法問題を解いてつまずいたら、何度も読み直すようにしましょう。また繰り返し同じ単語を目にしたり聞いたりすることで語彙力も身につきます。たくさんの英語にできるだけ頻繁にふれるようにしましょう。

2．音読練習をしながら単語を覚える

　文章の中でその単語がどのように使われているかを意識しながら単語を暗記するようにしましょう。文章を音読しながら、その文章の中で使われている単語を覚えるという方法が望ましいです。本書のUnit 1－5のREADING PART 2や、Unit 6以降のPart 5, 6は穴埋め問題になっています。これらのパートで出てきた文章に、正解の選択肢の語彙を入れて音読すると、文法と語彙の復習ができ、一石二鳥になります。

　一文を音読し終えた後に、日本語でその文章の訳を言う練習を繰り返すと、単語の意味が自然と頭に入ってきます。正しい単語の読み方を理解していれば、その知識はリスニング・セクションでも活かされます。

Unit 5 Personnel

Listening Section

 Before Listening

☑ Vocabulary check

Choose the correct meaning for each word or phrase.

1. apply for   (   )   2. CEO   (   )
3. fill out   (   )   4. full-time   (   )
5. human resources   (   )   6. résumé   (   )

記入する	正社員の	履歴書
最高経営責任者（取締役、社長）	応募する	人事部

🎧 18 Part 1 Four Pictures

You will see a set of four pictures, and you will hear one short phrase or sentence. Look at the set of pictures. Choose the picture that the phrase or sentence best describes.

1.

(A)   (B)

2.

(A)   (B)

(C)   (D)

(C)   (D)

Ⓐ Ⓑ Ⓒ Ⓓ

34

Part 2 Question-Response

You will hear some questions or statements. After each question or statement, you will hear and read four responses. Choose the best response to each question or statement.

3. (A) No, I don't like it.
   (B) It was last week.
   (C) OK, please fill out this form.
   (D) Me neither.

   Ⓐ Ⓑ Ⓒ Ⓓ

4. (A) I'm from Toronto.
   (B) It looks nice.
   (C) That's a good idea.
   (D) It's just over there.

   Ⓐ Ⓑ Ⓒ Ⓓ

Part 3 Conversation

You will hear a short conversation. You will hear and read two questions about the conversation. Each question has four answer choices. Choose the best answer to each question.

5. Who is the woman?
   (A) An applicant
   (B) A part-timer
   (C) An office staff
   (D) An interviewer

   Ⓐ Ⓑ Ⓒ Ⓓ

6. What does the woman want to do?
   (A) Attend a conference
   (B) Find a full-time position
   (C) Get a part-time job
   (D) Fill out the form

   Ⓐ Ⓑ Ⓒ Ⓓ

Part 4 Talk

You will hear a short talk. You will hear and read two questions about each talk. The question has four answer choices. Choose the best answer to each question.

7. **What does the woman ask the audience to do?**
   (A) Introduce themselves
   (B) Turn off their mobile phones
   (C) Make a speech
   (D) Switch on their mobile phones

   Ⓐ Ⓑ Ⓒ Ⓓ

8. **What will the woman do next?**
   (A) Introduce someone
   (B) Make a speech
   (C) Switch on her mobile phone
   (D) Attend another conference

   Ⓐ Ⓑ Ⓒ Ⓓ

📖 Reading Section

♠ *Before Reading*

☑ Vocabulary check

Choose the correct meaning for each word or phrase.

1. assemble	(	)	2. audience	(	)
3. board member	(	)	4. inspect	(	)
5. wage	(	)	6. paid vacation	(	)

役員	聴衆	検査する
給料	有給休暇	組み立てる

■ 受動態 ■

●受動態の意味

受動態の文は、日本語の「～される」を意味し、それに対して「～する」にあたる文は「能動態」と呼ばれています。

●受動態の形

受動態では、動詞が「be動詞＋動詞の過去分詞形」の形をとります。動詞の過去分詞形は、規則動詞には -edをつけますが、不規則動詞の過去分詞形は語によって違います。巻末の不規則動詞の一覧表を覚えるようにしてください。

〈能動態〉

（**例**）The staff uses this laptop computer.
   主語 動詞 目的語

  （スタッフはこのノート型パソコンを使います。）

〈受動態〉

（**例**）This laptop computer is used by the staff.
    主語   be＋過去分詞 by＋目的語

  （このノート型パソコンはスタッフによって使われています。）

●感情を表す受動態

感情を表現するときに、英語では受動態を使います。

（**例**）I was surprised at the news.（私はそのニュースに驚きました。）

surprisedは「（人）を驚かす」という意味の語なので、驚かされる側が主語になる場合は受動態になります。

その他の例

be satisfied with（満足する） be disappointed at（がっかりする）

be interested in（興味を持つ） be excited about（またはat）（わくわくする）

（**例題**）We ＿＿＿＿＿＿＿ at the sales profit.

  (A) disappointed (B) disappoint (C) are disappointing (D) are disappointed

（**解答**）(D) are disappointed（私たちは売上利益にがっかりしました。）

  disappointは「私たち」の感情を表す語なので、受動態を用います。したがって、be動詞＋過去分詞形をとる (D) が正解になります。

Choose the correct word to complete each sentence.

(1)   All the students are _____ from entering this room.
      (A) prohibit   (B) prohibited   Ⓐ Ⓑ

(2)   If you are not _____ with our product, our company will refund the full price.
      (A) satisfied   (B) satisfy   Ⓐ Ⓑ

Part 1 Sentence Completion

**You will read some sentences. Each one has a space where a word or phrase is missing.
Choose the best answer to complete the sentence.**

9.   The audience _____ with the speech.
     (A) were boring
     (B) was bored
     (C) boring
     (D) bore   Ⓐ Ⓑ Ⓒ Ⓓ

10. The earthquake _____ some industries.
     (A) were affected
     (B) was affected
     (C) affect
     (D) affected   Ⓐ Ⓑ Ⓒ Ⓓ

11. He sent a gift to his client, but it was _____ to his office.
     (A) return
     (B) returned
     (C) returns
     (D) returning   Ⓐ Ⓑ Ⓒ Ⓓ

12. The board members _____ to offer bonuses to employees.
     (A) were decided
     (B) be decided
     (C) decided
     (D) deciding   Ⓐ Ⓑ Ⓒ Ⓓ

Part 2 Text Completion

You will read a short text. Each one has three spaces where a word, phrase, or sentence is missing. For each space, choose the best answer to complete the text.

GT Electronics is —(13)— an accountant. —(14)—, please visit our website and download the application forms. —(15)—, send the forms to application@career.com.

13. (A) starting at
    (B) picking up
    (C) looking for
    (D) seeking after
          Ⓐ Ⓑ Ⓒ Ⓓ

14. (A) If you are interested in this position
    (B) When you get an e-mail from the accountant
    (C) After you fill in the form
    (D) Before visiting your company
          Ⓐ Ⓑ Ⓒ Ⓓ

15. (A) Before that
    (B) After all
    (C) Then
    (D) At last
          Ⓐ Ⓑ Ⓒ Ⓓ

You will read a text. Choose the best answer to each question.

Questions 16 - 18 refer to the following advertisement.

JOBS

Experienced Mechanics NEEDED

EPTCo Industries is seeking workers for our electronic parts factory.

Responsibilities include:
• Sorting electronic parts
• Assembling electronic equipment
• Inspecting products
• Shipping parts

This is a full-time position with wages paid hourly. Benefits include full medical insurance and paid vacations. E-mail for details: mariay@eptco-jobs.com

---

16. **Who is the factory seeking?**
    (A) Inexperienced mechanics
    (B) Experienced engineers
    (C) Full-time workers
    (D) Part-time workers   Ⓐ Ⓑ Ⓒ Ⓓ

17. **What is NOT a responsibility of the job?**
    (A) Checking products
    (B) Sorting out parts
    (C) Packing products
    (D) Putting equipment together   Ⓐ Ⓑ Ⓒ Ⓓ

18. **What benefits are included?**
    (A) Hourly breaks
    (B) Paid time off
    (C) Free vacation trips
    (D) Medical training   Ⓐ Ⓑ Ⓒ Ⓓ

column

TOEIC® L&R Test学習法（リーディング編）

　TOEIC® L&R Testを初めて受験した学習者からよく、「リーディング（Part 7）が全然できなかった」という声を耳にします。問題の多さや文章の長さに圧倒され、短い時間で解かなければならないというプレッシャーにより、普段の実力が発揮できなかったのかもしれません。読解問題を効率よく解くにはどのような練習をすればよいのでしょうか。

1．まずはタイトルを見て、主題が何であるかを確認する

　TOEIC Bridge® L&R TestsとTOEIC® L&R Testの読解問題では、多くの場合、広告文やニュースの見出し、Eメールの件名などのタイトルがついています。まずそこに注目すれば主題が何であるかを比較的簡単に理解することができます。タイトルがない場合でも、1文目か2文目でたいてい主題が書かれています。また誰に向けてその文章が書かれているかを理解することも要点をつかむ上で大切です。

2．設問を一読して意味を理解する

　読解問題に対するすべての設問を一読したら、一旦テキストを閉じて、何が問われていたかを日本語で声に出して言ってみてください。日本語で内容が言えないならば、設問を「見ていた」だけで「理解した」とは言えません。本番のテストで設問を何度も読み返すと、その分時間のロスになりますので、設問の意味が瞬時に理解できるように普段から練習しておくとよいでしょう。

3．長文の中から答えを探し出す

　1文目から最後の文章まで全部を読もうとする必要はありません。もちろん、短い広告文、表、グラフであれば、隅々まで見る必要がありますが、そうでない限りは、必要な情報だけを探して読むようにしてください。設問を読んだ際に記憶した大事なキーワード（長文の中で出てくると思われる表現や数字、固有名詞など）を探すつもりで、英文全体を見てください。そして、その単語が目に入ったら、その前後をしっかり読んで、答えにつながる情報を探し出します。その際に選択肢と照らし合わせながら読むと早く答えが見つかります。

　このような方法で普段から読解問題を解くように心がけると、短時間で解けるようになり、瞬時に主題や要点がつかめるようになってきます。

🎧 Listening Section

👆 *Before Listening*

☑ Vocabulary check

Choose the correct meaning for each word or phrase.

1. construction site (   )   **2.** check out   (   )
3. clothing store   (   )   **4.** enter   (   )
5. item   (   )   **6.** laptop computer (   )
7. mark down   (   )   **8.** shelf   (   )

調べる	入る	洋服屋	商品
ノート型パソコン	値下げする	工事現場	棚

🎧 22 Part 1 Photographs

You will hear four statements about a picture. Select the one statement that best describes what you see in the picture.

1.

Ⓐ Ⓑ Ⓒ Ⓓ

2.

Ⓐ Ⓑ Ⓒ Ⓓ

Part 2 Question-Response

You will hear a question or statement and three responses. Select the best response to the question or statement.

3. Mark your answer on your answer sheet.
   (A) (B) (C)

4. Mark your answer on your answer sheet.
   (A) (B) (C)

5. Mark your answer on your answer sheet.
   (A) (B) (C)

Part 3 Conversation

You will hear a conversation between two or more people. You will be asked to answer three questions about what the speakers say in the conversation. Select the best response to each question.

6. **Where are the speakers?**
   (A) In a bookstore
   (B) In a movie theater
   (C) In a clothing store
   (D) In a station
   (A) (B) (C) (D)

7. **Who is the man?**
   (A) A shop clerk
   (B) A client
   (C) An engineer
   (D) A conductor
   (A) (B) (C) (D)

8. **What is the woman looking for?**
   (A) Her skirt
   (B) Her daughter's clothes
   (C) Her mother's skirt
   (D) Her mother's shirt
   (A) (B) (C) (D)

You will hear a talk given by a single speaker. You will be asked to answer three questions about what the speaker says in the talk. Select the best response to each question.

9. **When does the sale begin?**
   (A) Wednesday
   (B) Thursday
   (C) Friday
   (D) Saturday   Ⓐ Ⓑ Ⓒ Ⓓ

10. **When does the store close during the sale?**
   (A) At 9:00 p.m.
   (B) At 10:00 p.m.
   (C) At 11:00 p.m.
   (D) At 12:00 a.m.   Ⓐ Ⓑ Ⓒ Ⓓ

11. **Look at the chart on the department website. Which item costs $30 during the sale?**
   (A) A coat
   (B) A travel bag
   (C) A pair of sports shoes
   (D) A handbag   Ⓐ Ⓑ Ⓒ Ⓓ

Item	Regular price
Spring coat	$90.00
Handbag	$60.00
Athletic shoes	$80.00
Travel bag	$70.00

📖 Reading Section

🖋 *Before Reading*

☑ Vocabulary check

Choose the correct meaning for each word.

1. coupon   (   )   **2.** delivery   (   )

3. due   (   )   **4.** expire   (   )

5. invoice   (   )   **6.** purchase   (   )

7. quantity   (   )   **8.** reply   (   )

配達	請求書	数量	期限が切れる
優待券	返事する	当然支払われるべきもの	購入

Grammar

■ 代名詞 ■

代名詞とは、名詞の代わりに使われ、名詞の繰り返しを避けます。例えば、my colleagues（私の同僚たち）が誰なのかがわかっている場合、they（彼ら、彼女ら）という表現に置き換えることができます。

		主格 （〜は）	所有格 （〜の）	目的格 （〜を、〜に）	所有代名詞 （〜のもの）	再帰代名詞 （〜自身）
単数	私	I	my	me	mine	myself
	あなた	you	your	you	yours	yourself
	彼	he	his	him	his	himself
	彼女	she	her	her	hers	herself
	それ	it	its	it		itself
複数	私たち	we	our	us	ours	ourselves
	あなたたち	you	your	you	yours	yourselves
	彼ら、彼女ら それら	they	their	them	theirs	themselves

● 「〜は」の列は、主語を代名詞に置き換える時に使います。

（例）My colleagues are all kind.（私の同僚はみんな親切です。）

下線部の My colleagues は、-s が付いているので複数形です。これを、代名詞を使って言い換えると「彼らは（彼女らは）」に相当するので、They are all kind. になります。

● 「〜の」の列は、所有を表現するときに使います。

（例）It is Tim's computer.（それはティムのパソコンです。）

Tim's computer（ティムのパソコン）を「彼の」パソコンと言いたいときは、「〜の」の列にある his を使って、It is his computer. と言い換えることができます。

● 「〜を、〜に」の列は、目的語を代名詞に置き換えるときに使います。

（例）I bought a watch.（私は時計を買いました。）

a watch（時計を）を「それを」と言い換えたいときは、「〜を、〜に」の列にある it を使って、I bought it. と言い換えることができます。

● 「〜のもの」の列は、次のような例文を言い換えるときに使います。

（例）This is my file.（これは私のファイルです。）

この文を「これは私のものです」と言い換えたいとき、「〜のもの」の列にある mine を使って、This is mine. と言い換えることができます。

● 「〜自身」という再帰代名詞は、代名詞に -self（複数形 -selves）が付いた形です。

（例）I fell down and hurt myself.（私は転んでけがをしました。）

hurt（〜を傷つける）という動作の対象が、自分自身に向けられています。

Choose the correct word to complete each sentence.

(1) _____ go to work by bus.
    (A) They   (B) Their   (A)(B)

(2) Mr. Franklin gave _____ a new assignment.
    (A) my   (B) me   (A)(B)

Part 5 Incomplete Sentences

A word or phrase is missing in each of the sentences. Select the best answer to complete the sentence.

12. Ms. Walker sent me an e-mail, and _____ replied to it yesterday.
    (A) myself
    (B) me
    (C) my
    (D) I   (A)(B)(C)(D)

13. How can I plan the entire conference by _____ ?
    (A) me
    (B) mine
    (C) myself
    (D) I   (A)(B)(C)(D)

14. You can take _____ lunch break in the break room.
    (A) you
    (B) your
    (C) her
    (D) hers   (A)(B)(C)(D)

15. It is hard for _____ to find a new job.
    (A) we
    (B) their
    (C) them
    (D) it   (A)(B)(C)(D)

Read the text that follows. A word, phrase, or sentence is missing in parts of the text. Select the best answer to complete the text.

Questions 16 - 19 refer to the following e-mail.

FROM: Revolution Clothing Ltd. <coupon@revclothing.com>
TO: Hans T. Perry <perry76@mnet.com>
SUBJECT: Coupon offer
DATE: November 7, 2019

Dear Customer,

Thank you for _____ clothing from the Revolution Clothing website. _____.
　　　　　　　　　16.　　　　　　　　　　　　　　　　　　　　　　　**17.**
To use your coupon, please visit www.revclothing.com and _____ your coupon
　　　　　　　　　　　　　　　　　　　　　　　　　　　　　　18.
code.

Enjoy your shopping _____ with Revolution Clothing.
　　　　　　　　　　　　19.

---

16. (A) purchase
    (B) purchases
    (C) purchased
    (D) purchasing
    Ⓐ Ⓑ Ⓒ Ⓓ

17. (A) We would like to give you this Internet coupon for your next purchase.
    (B) Please accept our apology for the delay of the delivery.
    (C) We sell a wide variety of food products.
    (D) Your membership card will expire in 30 days.
    Ⓐ Ⓑ Ⓒ Ⓓ

18. (A) buy
    (B) enter
    (C) suggest
    (D) vote
    Ⓐ Ⓑ Ⓒ Ⓓ

19. (A) experiment
    (B) expectation
    (C) explanation
    (D) experience
    Ⓐ Ⓑ Ⓒ Ⓓ

Read the following text. Select the best answer for each question.

Questions 20 - 22 refer to the following invoice.

Valu-Create

Weights and Gym Supplies

TO:

Mr. Peter Koren, Vice President
Gymbusters, Ltd.
32 St. Lawrence Street
Temple City, Nebraska, 13590
837-555-1532

Invoice # 621

Date placed: February 12, 2020

Shipping date: February 25, 2020

DESCRIPTION	QUANTITY	UNIT PRICE	TOTAL
Treadmills	4	$2027.00	$8108.00
Adjustable Weight Sets	25	$51.50	$1287.50
Weight Benches	6	$157.00	$942.00
Rowing Machine	1	$499.00	$499.00
		SUBTOTAL	$10,836.50
		SALES TAX	$162.55
		SHIPPING	
		TOTAL DUE	**$10,999.05**

20. **When was the order shipped?**
    (A) February 12
    (B) February 25
    (C) June 21
    (D) Not mentioned

21. **How much does a single weight bench cost?**
    (A) $6.00
    (B) $157.00
    (C) $942.00
    (D) $10,836.50

22. **How many rowing machines did Gymbusters, Ltd. order?**
    (A) One
    (B) Four
    (C) Six
    (D) Twenty-five

Advertisement

 Listening Section

👍 *Before Listening*

☑ **Vocabulary check**

Choose the correct meaning for each word or phrase.

1. advertise	(	)	**2.** beverage	(	)		
3. brochure	(	)	**4.** competitor	(	)		
5. customer	(	)	**6.** product	(	)		
7. reasonable	(	)	**8.** regular price	(	)		

通常価格	顧客	競争相手	飲み物
パンフレット	商品	（値段が）それほど高くない	広告する

🎧 [26] **Part 1** **Photographs**

You will hear four statements about a picture. Select the one statement that best describes what you see in the picture.

1.

2.

Ⓐ Ⓑ Ⓒ Ⓓ   Ⓐ Ⓑ Ⓒ Ⓓ

Part 2 Question-Response

You will hear a question or statement and three responses. Select the best response to the question or statement.

3. Mark your answer on your answer sheet.   Ⓐ Ⓑ Ⓒ

4. Mark your answer on your answer sheet.   Ⓐ Ⓑ Ⓒ

5. Mark your answer on your answer sheet.   Ⓐ Ⓑ Ⓒ

Part 3 Conversation

You will hear a conversation between two or more people. You will be asked to answer three questions about what the speakers say in the conversation. Select the best response to each question.

6. **What does the woman think about the brochure?**
   (A) She likes the design very much.
   (B) She wants to change the design by herself.
   (C) She wants Jason to change the design.
   (D) She needs it by next week.   Ⓐ Ⓑ Ⓒ Ⓓ

7. **How does the brochure look?**
   (A) Too similar to the last one
   (B) Too similar to their competitor's
   (C) Different from the last one
   (D) Different from their competitor's   Ⓐ Ⓑ Ⓒ Ⓓ

8. **What will the man do?**
   (A) Print the brochure
   (B) Hire a designer
   (C) Change the design
   (D) Look for a printer   Ⓐ Ⓑ Ⓒ Ⓓ

TOEIC®

7

Advertisement

You will hear a talk given by a single speaker. You will be asked to answer three questions about what the speaker says in the talk. Select the best response to each question.

9. **What is the advertisement for?**
   (A) An instant meal
   (B) A new beverage
   (C) A new supplement
   (D) A new tea
   Ⓐ Ⓑ Ⓒ Ⓓ

10. **What is convenient about the product?**
    (A) It is sold in vending machines.
    (B) It is sold in convenience stores.
    (C) It is easy to eat.
    (D) It is easy to carry.
    Ⓐ Ⓑ Ⓒ Ⓓ

11. **What is special about the product?**
    (A) Its nutritional value
    (B) Its mixed flavors
    (C) Its unique shape
    (D) Its reasonable price
    Ⓐ Ⓑ Ⓒ Ⓓ

📖 Reading Section

👆 *Before Reading*

☑ Vocabulary check

Choose the correct meaning for each word or phrase.

1. appliance store	( )	2. warranty	( )
3. criminal	( )	4. engineer	( )
5. furniture	( )	6. kitchen equipment	( )
7. occasion	( )	8. provide	( )

家庭用電気器具店	犯人	技師	家具
台所用品	保証	提供する	機会

■ 数えられる名詞、数えられない名詞 ■

名詞には、1つ、2つと数えられるもの（可算名詞）と、数えられないもの（不可算名詞）があります。例えば、pencilやdeskといった名詞は、a pencil（1本の鉛筆）、three pencils（3本の鉛筆）というように数えられるので、aや-sがつきますが、次に挙げる名詞は「抽象名詞（具体的な形がない抽象的なことを表す）」や「物質名詞（一定の形がない物質を表す）」と呼ばれ、1つ、2つと数えることができません。

抽象名詞	advice（助言） information（情報） knowledge（知識） kindness（優しさ）等
物質名詞	money（金）　furniture（家具）　paper（紙）　water（水）等

●注意が必要な名詞

- news（複数形に見えますが、単数扱いをします。）

  （例）The news **was** shocking.（そのニュースは衝撃的でした。）

- police（単数形に見えますが、複数扱いをします。）

  （例）The police **are** after him.（警察は彼を追っています。）

（例題 1）For _____, please contact us by e-mail.

    (A) informations　　　　(B) an information

    (C) more information　　　(D) many information

（解答）(C) more information（詳細はEメールで私たちにお問い合わせください。）
数えられない名詞の例にも挙げたように、information は数えられません。したがって、単数を表す a がついたり、複数を表す -s がついたりすることはありません。また many は数えられる名詞の前だけにつくので (D) も不正解になります。

（例題 2）Economics _____ a social science that analyzes the economic trends.

    (A) is　　　　(B) was　　　　(C) are　　　　(D) were

（解答）(A) is（経済学とは経済動向を分析する社会科学です。）
economics（経済学）という語のように学問を表す名詞で語尾が-icsのものは、単数として扱います。したがって、be動詞は is か was のどちらかに絞ることができます。この文は、一般的に経済学とはどのような学問であるかを説明しているので、時制は過去形にはなりません。そのため現在形の (A) が正解になります。

右側欄外：

TOEIC®

7

Advertisement

Choose the correct word to complete each sentence.

(1) Mathematics _____ the most important subject for most engineers.

    (A) is   (B) are   Ⓐ Ⓑ

(2) We have to buy new office _____.

    (A) furniture   (B) furnitures   Ⓐ Ⓑ

Part 5 Incomplete Sentences

A word or phrase is missing in each of the sentences. Select the best answer to complete the sentence.

12. The police _____ searching for the criminal.

    (A) is

    (B) are

    (C) was

    (D) being   Ⓐ Ⓑ Ⓒ Ⓓ

13. I want to buy some kitchen _____.

    (A) equipment

    (B) equipments

    (C) equipped

    (D) equip   Ⓐ Ⓑ Ⓒ Ⓓ

14. After my presentation, please give me your _____.

    (A) advise

    (B) advises

    (C) advice

    (D) advices   Ⓐ Ⓑ Ⓒ Ⓓ

15. Labor _____ were very high, so my boss was very angry about it.

    (A) costs

    (B) cost

    (C) costing

    (D) coasted   Ⓐ Ⓑ Ⓒ Ⓓ

Read the text that follows. A word, phrase, or sentence is missing in parts of the text. Select the best answer to complete the text.

Questions 16 - 19 refer to the following advertisement.

> We are happy to announce that we are _____ a new model of
>
> **16.**
>
> dishwasher this spring. Not only is our new Whirlmaster 3000 dishwasher
>
> very quiet, but it also makes dishwashing _____ than ever. With
>
> **17.**
>
> special racks and cup holders, you'll be able to wash dishes _____.
>
> **18.**
>
> The Whirlmaster 3000 comes in white and silver colors, and has a three-
>
> year warranty. _____.
>
> **19.**

16. (A) being released
    (B) released
    (C) releasing
    (D) release

    Ⓐ Ⓑ Ⓒ Ⓓ

17. (A) easy
    (B) easier
    (C) easiest
    (D) easily

    Ⓐ Ⓑ Ⓒ Ⓓ

18. (A) quick
    (B) quicken
    (C) quickness
    (D) quickly

    Ⓐ Ⓑ Ⓒ Ⓓ

19. (A) Press the white button to start.
    (B) Hurry up and get a new washing machine.
    (C) It won't be available until next spring.
    (D) You can purchase it at most appliance stores.

    Ⓐ Ⓑ Ⓒ Ⓓ

Read the following text. Select the best answer for each question.

Questions 20 - 22 refer to the following advertisement.

Kingston Catering

For all your catering needs

We are ready to cater for your office party, wedding, or special event. We offer a wide selection of food including delicious organic and vegetable dishes.

We also provide a wide selection of beverages, including imported fine wines. We can also help you find the perfect place for your special occasion.

Kingston Catering is here for all your catering needs

Call us: 415-555-465

Hours: 9:00 a.m. - 8:00 p.m., Monday to Friday

To receive online discounts, visit our website: www.kingstoncatering.com

---

20. What information does NOT appear in the advertisement?

(A) The kinds of service the company offers

(B) E-mail address

(C) Phone number

(D) The company's business hours   Ⓐ Ⓑ Ⓒ Ⓓ

21. On what occasion do customers most likely order from the company?

(A) On a move-out day

(B) On a business trip

(C) At a party

(D) At a job interview   Ⓐ Ⓑ Ⓒ Ⓓ

22. **How can customers get a discount?**

(A) By phoning the office

(B) By visiting the office

(C) By choosing extra services

(D) By visiting the website

Unit 8 Daily Life

 ## Listening Section

🖐 *Before Listening*

☑ Vocabulary check

Choose the correct meaning for each word or phrase.

1.	electronics store	(	)	**2.**	fragile	(	)
3.	make up one's mind	(	)	**4.**	package	(	)
5.	return	(	)	**6.**	temperature	(	)
7.	turn on	(	)	**8.**	weather forecast	(	)

小包	気温	天気予報	～のスイッチを入れる
戻る	決心する	壊れやすい	電気店

🎧 **30** **Part 1 Photographs**

You will hear four statements about a picture. Select the one statement that best describes what you see in the picture.

1.

Ⓐ Ⓑ Ⓒ Ⓓ

2.

Ⓐ Ⓑ Ⓒ Ⓓ

58

Part **2** Question-Response

You will hear a question or statement and three responses. Select the best response to the question or statement.

3. Mark your answer on your answer sheet.   Ⓐ Ⓑ Ⓒ

4. Mark your answer on your answer sheet.   Ⓐ Ⓑ Ⓒ

5. Mark your answer on your answer sheet.   Ⓐ Ⓑ Ⓒ

Part **3** Conversation

You will hear a conversation between two or more people. You will be asked to answer three questions about what the speakers say in the conversation. Select the best response to each question.

6. Where does this conversation probably take place?
   - (A) At a post office
   - (B) At a bank
   - (C) At a hotel
   - (D) At an electronics store   Ⓐ Ⓑ Ⓒ Ⓓ

7. What is inside the package?
   - (A) A desktop computer
   - (B) A battery
   - (C) A mobile phone
   - (D) A laptop computer   Ⓐ Ⓑ Ⓒ Ⓓ

8. What will the woman do next?
   - (A) Go to Germany
   - (B) Go to an electronics store
   - (C) Fill in the form
   - (D) Open the package   Ⓐ Ⓑ Ⓒ Ⓓ

TOEIC®

8

Daily Life

You will hear a talk given by a single speaker. You will be asked to answer three questions about what the speaker says in the talk. Select the best response to each question.

9. **What is the man's occupation?**

    (A) A film director

    (B) A scientist

    (C) A weather forecaster

    (D) A commentator   Ⓐ Ⓑ Ⓒ Ⓓ

10. **What is the temperature tonight?**

    (A) 10 degrees

    (B) 16 degrees

    (C) 18 degrees

    (D) 40 degrees   Ⓐ Ⓑ Ⓒ Ⓓ

11. **When will it be cloudy?**

    (A) This evening

    (B) Tonight

    (C) Tomorrow

    (D) The day after tomorrow   Ⓐ Ⓑ Ⓒ Ⓓ

📖 Reading Section

♦ *Before Reading*

☑ Vocabulary check

Choose the correct meaning for each word or phrase.

1.	auditorium	(	)	2.	complete	(	)
3.	discounted price	(	)	4.	enclose	(	)
5.	farewell party	(	)	6.	fine	(	)
7.	replacement	(	)	8.	resident	(	)

罰金	交換の品	送別会	割引価格
同封する	完了する	居住者	ホール

■ 数量詞 ■

数量詞とは、次の表に示されるように、数量を表す語のことで、名詞の前に置かれ、その名詞を修飾します。

		可算名詞	不可算名詞
a few	少しの	○	
many	多くの	○	
a little	少しの		○
much	多くの		○
a lot of	多くの	○	○

※ few, little は共に「ほとんど〜ない」という否定の意味になります。例えば、I have little money. の場合（私はほとんどお金を持っていません）という意味になりますが、I have a little money. の場合は（私は少しだけお金を持っています）という意味になります。

数量詞には以下のようなものもあり、単数形にしか使われないものや、複数形にしか使われないものがあります。

		単数形	複数形	不可算名詞
all	すべての	○	○	○
another	もう一つの	○		
both	両方の		○	
each	それぞれの	○		
every	すべての	○		
several	いくつかの		○	
some, any	いくつかの	○	○	○

（例）Please show me another example.
　　　（もう一つ別の例を示してください。）
another の後に続く名詞には -s がつかず、複数形にはなりません。

（例）Every country has its laws.
　　　（どんな国にもそれぞれの法があります。）
every は「すべての」という意味で、「国」が複数にあることを前提としていますが、countriesという複数名詞にはなりません。everyの後に続く名詞は必ず単数形になるので注意しましょう。

Choose the correct word to complete each sentence.

(1) _____ the books are sold at discounted prices.

    (A) Most of   (B) Most   Ⓐ Ⓑ

(2) It will take _____ days for the shipment.

    (A) another   (B) several   Ⓐ Ⓑ

Part 5 Incomplete Sentences

A word or phrase is missing in each of the sentences. Select the best answer to complete the sentence.

12. Would you like _____ more coffee?

    (A) many

    (B) some

    (C) several

    (D) another   Ⓐ Ⓑ Ⓒ Ⓓ

13. _____ brand names are very popular among young ladies.

    (A) Every

    (B) Each

    (C) All of

    (D) Both   Ⓐ Ⓑ Ⓒ Ⓓ

14. Ms. Green drank too _____ wine at the farewell party.

    (A) many

    (B) much

    (C) lot of

    (D) many of   Ⓐ Ⓑ Ⓒ Ⓓ

15. There are _____ people in the auditorium.

    (A) few

    (B) little

    (C) much

    (D) every   Ⓐ Ⓑ Ⓒ Ⓓ

Part **6** Text Completion

Read the text that follows. A word, phrase, or sentence is missing in parts of the text.
Select the best answer to complete the text.

Questions 16 - 19 refer to the following letter.

Alexandra Deacon-Jones
21 Leonard Road, Apt. 119
Gardena, California 74436

February 19, 2020
Dear Ms. Deacon-Jones,

As you may already know, Alpine Villas will _____ ownership and become
                          16.
part of Hamilton National Home's chain of _____ apartments this March.
                                     17.
I will send all residents more _____ when the change has been completed.
                         18.

_____.
  19.
Sincerely,
Edward Burton
Alpine Villas Administration

16. (A) change
    (B) be changed
    (C) to change
    (D) changing   Ⓐ Ⓑ Ⓒ Ⓓ

17. (A) resident
    (B) residents
    (C) residential
    (D) residentially   Ⓐ Ⓑ Ⓒ Ⓓ

18. (A) information
    (B) presents
    (C) complaints
    (D) money   Ⓐ Ⓑ Ⓒ Ⓓ

19. (A) For details, please check with your family members.
    (B) Please let us know if you can attend the meeting.
    (C) The deadline for the application is March 31.
    (D) If you have any questions, please contact us.   Ⓐ Ⓑ Ⓒ Ⓓ

TOEIC®

8

Daily Life

Read the following texts. Select the best answer for each question.

Questions 20 - 24 refer to the following letters.

September 5, 2020

Dear Ms. Jeannette Davis:

I am writing to inform you that the book you checked out, *The Darkest Night* by Philip Ellis, is three months overdue. We will not charge you if the book is returned to the Makah Central Library right away. If there is any further delay, you will need to pay a $20 fine.

If you have lost the book, the replacement fee is $30. If the book is not returned, your library membership will be canceled.

Yours sincerely,

Jerome Watson

Head Librarian
Makah Central Library

Dear Mr. Watson,

I'm sorry for failing to return the book. I moved out of town two weeks ago, and I am now living in nearby Georgetown.

I haven't had a chance to take the book back to the library. I've enclosed the book in this package instead.

Yours sincerely,

Jeannette Davis

20. **What is the purpose of Mr. Watson's letter to Ms. Davis?**
    (A) To remind her that her book is overdue
    (B) To ask her to be a library member
    (C) To reply to her request for an interview
    (D) To ask her to join a popular book club

21. **When did Ms. Davis have to return the book?**
    (A) September 5
    (B) Three months ago
    (C) Two weeks ago
    (D) 20 days ago

22. **Why did Ms. Davis NOT return the book?**
    (A) She wanted to keep the book.
    (B) She lost the book.
    (C) Her library membership was canceled.
    (D) She no longer lives in the same town.

23. **How much is the replacement fee?**
    (A) Free
    (B) $20
    (C) $30
    (D) $50

24. **What did Ms. Davis send with the letter?**
    (A) $20 fine
    (B) $30 fee
    (C) The book
    (D) The library card

9 Office Work

TOEIC®

🎧 Listening Section

☝ *Before Listening*

☑ Vocabulary check

Choose the correct meaning for each word or phrase.

1. be located	(	)	**2.** caller	(	)
3. drop by	(	)	**4.** fix	(	)
5. jam	(	)	**6.** make copies	(	)
7. (be) on duty	(	)	**8.** weekday	(	)

〜に立ち寄る	コピーを取る	平日	勤務時間中で
電話をかける人	修理する	位置する	詰まらせる

🎧34 Part **1** Photographs

You will hear four statements about a picture. Select the one statement that best describes what you see in the picture.

1.

2.

 Ⓐ Ⓑ Ⓒ Ⓓ    Ⓐ Ⓑ Ⓒ Ⓓ

Part 2 Question-Response

You will hear a question or statement and three responses. Select the best response to the question or statement.

3. Mark your answer on your answer sheet. Ⓐ Ⓑ Ⓒ

4. Mark your answer on your answer sheet. Ⓐ Ⓑ Ⓒ

5. Mark your answer on your answer sheet. Ⓐ Ⓑ Ⓒ

Part 3 Conversation

You will hear a conversation between two or more people. You will be asked to answer three questions about what the speakers say in the conversation. Select the best response to each question.

6. **Why was the man not in the office?**
   (A) He was in a meeting.
   (B) He was having lunch.
   (C) He was sick at home.
   (D) He was having a job interview. Ⓐ Ⓑ Ⓒ Ⓓ

7. **What does the woman tell the man?**
   (A) The caller's name
   (B) The boss's name
   (C) The caller's phone number
   (D) Her phone number Ⓐ Ⓑ Ⓒ Ⓓ

8. **Look at the memo. What will the man probably do next?**
   (A) Give a memo to the woman
   (B) Call Alfred before the afternoon meeting
   (C) Drop by Alfred's office
   (D) Call Alfred after 3 p.m. Ⓐ Ⓑ Ⓒ Ⓓ

> **Memo**
> Date: Nov 11, 2019   Time: 12:30
> - Call from Alfred Butler
> - Alfred's afternoon meeting time 2 p.m-3 p.m.

Part 4 Talk

You will hear a talk given by a single speaker. You will be asked to answer three questions about what the speaker says in the talk. Select the best response to each question.

9. **Where is the parking area located?**
   (A) In front of this building
   (B) Next to this building
   (C) At the back of this building
   (D) Across the street from the building   Ⓐ Ⓑ Ⓒ Ⓓ

10. **What do people show to the guard?**
   (A) Their member's card
   (B) Their badge
   (C) Their wallet
   (D) Their fingerprint   Ⓐ Ⓑ Ⓒ Ⓓ

11. **When is the guard NOT in the parking area?**
   (A) Monday at 8:00 a.m.
   (B) Thursday at 8:00 p.m.
   (C) Saturday at 9:00 a.m.
   (D) Sunday at 9:00 a.m.   Ⓐ Ⓑ Ⓒ Ⓓ

📖 Reading Section

☝ *Before Reading*

☑ Vocabulary check

Choose the correct meaning for each word or phrase.

1. assistant manager ( )	2. establish ( )
3. employee ( )	4. extend ( )
5. funding ( )	6. in regards to ( )
7. institution ( )	8. overtime payment ( )

確立する	延長する	～に関して	残業手当
係長	財政的支援	施設	従業員

■ To不定詞 ■

●To不定詞の形

「to＋動詞の原形」

●To不定詞の意味

1. 名詞的用法「〜すること」

   I like to watch TV. (私はテレビを見ることが好きです。)

2. 形容詞的用法「〜するための」(名詞を修飾する)

   These are the samples to show our customers. (これらは、顧客に見せるためのサンプルです。)

3. 副詞的用法

   - 「〜するために」(目的を表す)

     He studied hard to enter the university. (彼はその大学に入るために一生懸命勉強しました。)

   - 「〜した結果…」(結果を表す)

     She grew up to be a lawyer. (彼女は成長して弁護士になりました。)

   - 「〜して」(原因・理由を表す)

     I was surprised to hear that. (私はそれを聞いて驚きました。)

●To不定詞を目的語にする動詞

動詞の中には、以下のように不定詞だけを目的語に取るものがあります。

agree (同意する)	ask (たずねる)	decide (決意する)
desire (強く願う)	expect (期待する)	promise (約束する)
refuse (拒否する)	want (欲しいと思う)	wish (望む)

(例題) I hope ＿＿＿＿＿＿ in Tokyo.

(A) live　　(B) living　　(C) to live　　(D) be living

(解答) (C) to live (私は東京に住むことを望んでいます。)

hopeは上に挙げた「To不定詞を目的語にする動詞」のうちの1つです。したがって、hopeの後にはTo不定詞 (to＋動詞の原形) が置かれるので、正解は(C)になります。

Choose the correct word to complete each sentence.

(1) The Goodsleep Group decided _____ its market.
   (A) expanding   (B) to expand   Ⓐ Ⓑ

(2) The company desires _____ a good public image.
   (A) establishing   (B) to establish   Ⓐ Ⓑ

Part 5 Incomplete Sentences

A word or phrase is missing in each of the sentences. Select the best answer to complete the sentence.

12. The meeting gave the employees the chance _____ about their problems.
   (A) talks
   (B) talked
   (C) talking
   (D) to talk   Ⓐ Ⓑ Ⓒ Ⓓ

13. Everyone refuses _____ the fax machine.
   (A) using
   (B) to use
   (C) being used
   (D) to be using   Ⓐ Ⓑ Ⓒ Ⓓ

14. The supervisor told the staff _____ the company before 5 p.m.
   (A) not to leave
   (B) do not leave
   (C) to leave not
   (D) not leave   Ⓐ Ⓑ Ⓒ Ⓓ

15. Ms. Pak wants to _____ promoted to assistant manager.
   (A) be
   (B) are
   (C) were
   (D) does   Ⓐ Ⓑ Ⓒ Ⓓ

Read the text that follows. A word or phrase is missing in some of the sentences. Select the best answer to complete the text.

Questions 16 - 19 refer to the following notice.

To: Electro-Mart employees
From: Mark C. Gonzalez
Subject: Extended hours

To All Employees,

_____ on December 1, we will extend our business hours for the holiday
    16.
shopping season. Monday _____ Sunday, we will open one hour earlier
          17.
and close two hours _____ than usual, making our weekday hours 9:00
       18.
a.m. to 10:00 p.m. and our weekend hours 8:00 a.m. to 11:00 p.m. _____.
                 19.

Sincerely,
Mark C. Gonzalez

---

16. (A) Pressing   (B) Returning
    (C) Beginning   (D) Going

Ⓐ Ⓑ Ⓒ Ⓓ

17. (A) from   (B) through
    (C) between   (D) on

Ⓐ Ⓑ Ⓒ Ⓓ

18. (A) late   (B) later
    (C) latter   (D) latest

Ⓐ Ⓑ Ⓒ Ⓓ

19. (A) I hope you enjoy your holiday shopping.
    (B) Thank you very much for your purchase.
    (C) Therefore, all employees are not allowed to work overtime.
    (D) Any employees who work more than 40 hours a week will receive overtime
       payment.

Ⓐ Ⓑ Ⓒ Ⓓ

Read the following text. Select the best answer for each question.

Questions 20 - 22 refer to the following memorandum.

MEMO

TO:
Dr. Charles Pierce
FROM:
Mr. Grey, Cristic Institution

Message:
Please call Mr. Adrian Grey at his office as soon as you can, in regards to the project funding at the Cristic Institution. He says you applied for the funding. He wants you to inform him of the lab equipment requirements. Mr. Grey's office number: 202-555-1111.

Message taken by:
Jeff Walker, front office

20. **What does Mr. Grey want to know?**

(A) Specific requirements
(B) An appointment date
(C) Mr. Grey's office number
(D) Deadline for application

21. **Who applied for funding?**

(A) Jeff Walker
(B) Adrian Grey
(C) Charles Pierce
(D) A secretary

22. **What will Mr. Pierce probably do next?**

    (A) Go to Mr. Grey's office

    (B) Check his e-mail

    (C) Make a call

    (D) Take a coffee break

TOEIC®

9

Office Work

10 Business

🎧 Listening Section

✋ *Before Listening*

☑ Vocabulary check

Choose the correct meaning for each word or phrase.

1. make an appointment (	)	**2.** calculator (	)
3. be expected to do (	)	**4.** contract (	)
5. leave for (	)	**6.** look over (	)
7. messy (	)	**8.** plant (	)

散らかった	約束をする	計算機	～に向かって出発する
工場	～にざっと目を通す	～することになっている	契約書

🎧38 Part **1** Photographs

You will hear four statements about a picture. Select the one statement that best describes what you see in the picture.

1.

Ⓐ Ⓑ Ⓒ Ⓓ

2.

Ⓐ Ⓑ Ⓒ Ⓓ

You will hear a question or statement and three responses. Select the best response to the question or statement.

3. Mark your answer on your answer sheet.

4. Mark your answer on your answer sheet. (A) (B) (C)

5. Mark your answer on your answer sheet. (A) (B) (C)

40 **Part** 3 Conversation

You will hear a conversation between two or more people. You will be asked to answer three questions about what the speakers say in the conversation. Select the best response to each question.

6. **Where does this conversation probably take place?**
   (A) At home
   (B) In an office
   (C) At a restaurant
   (D) In a gym   (A) (B) (C) (D)

7. **What is in the filing cabinet?**
   (A) Books
   (B) The woman's lunch
   (C) Files
   (D) Contracts   (A) (B) (C) (D)

8. **What will the woman do?**
   (A) Leave the cabinet
   (B) File documents
   (C) Read the contracts
   (D) Have dinner   (A) (B) (C) (D)

TOEIC®

10

Business

You will hear a talk given by a single speaker. You will be asked to answer three questions about what the speaker says in the talk. Select the best response to each question.

9. **What product will the factory produce?**
   (A) Sports drinks
   (B) Chewing gum
   (C) Rubber bands
   (D) Green tea snacks   Ⓐ Ⓑ Ⓒ Ⓓ

10. **Where will the products be sold?**
    (A) Only in the U.S.
    (B) Only in Russia
    (C) In Asia
    (D) In Europe   Ⓐ Ⓑ Ⓒ Ⓓ

11. **When will the factory be completed?**
    (A) By the end of the month
    (B) Early next year
    (C) At the end of this year
    (D) In two years   Ⓐ Ⓑ Ⓒ Ⓓ

📖 Reading Section

🖋 *Before Reading*

☑ Vocabulary check

Choose the correct meaning for each word or phrase.

1. decline	(	)	2. demand	(	)
3. feature	(	)	4. increase	(	)
5. launch	(	)	6. responsibility	(	)
7. sacrifice	(	)	8. urban	(	)

需要	販売を開始する	増やす	減少
特色となる	犠牲にする	責任	都会の

Grammar

■ **動名詞** ■

● **動名詞の形**

「動詞の原形＋ -ing」

● **動名詞の意味**

「～すること」（名詞の働きをする）

● **動名詞を目的語にする動詞**

動詞の中には、以下のように動名詞だけを目的語に取るものがあります。

admit	（認める）	avoid	（避ける）	consider	（考慮する）
deny	（否定する）	enjoy	（楽しむ）	finish	（終える）
give up	（あきらめる）	mind	（気にする）	quit	（辞める）
put off	（延期する）				

● **不定詞と動名詞を目的語にする動詞**

不定詞と動名詞の両方を目的語に取れますが、どちらを取るかで意味が異なる語があります。例えば次のようなものがあります。

・ stop

    I stopped smoking.（私は煙草を吸うのをやめました。）

    I stopped to smoke.（私は煙草を吸うために立ち止まりました。）

stop の後に -ing を置いた場合、stop は「やめる」という意味になりますが、to do を置いた場合は「立ち止まる」という意味になります。

・ -ing と to do の意味的な違い

-ing は、stopped smoking（＜主語（人）＞は煙草を吸うのをやめました）や remember(s) seeing her（＜主語（人）＞は彼女に会ったことを覚えています）のように、すでに起きた過去のことを表しますが、to do は、stopped to smoke（＜主語（人）＞は煙草を吸うために立ち止まりました）や remember(s) to turn off the computer（＜主語（人）＞はコンピュータの電源を忘れず切ります）のように、これから起きる未来のことを表します。

・ remember

    I remember seeing her.

    （私は彼女に会ったことを覚えています。）

    Please remember to turn off the computer.

    （コンピュータの電源を忘れずに切ってください。）

remember の後に -ing を置いた場合、「～したことを覚えている」という意味になりますが、to do を置いた場合は「～することを覚えている、忘れずに～する」という意味になります。

TOEIC®

10

Business

Choose the correct word to complete each sentence.

(1) Most food chains stopped _____ Ethiopian coffee.
(A) to buy   (B) buying   Ⓐ Ⓑ

(2) _____ a business in an urban place takes a lot of effort.
(A) Establishing   (B) Established   Ⓐ Ⓑ

Part 5 Incomplete Sentences

A word or phrase is missing in each of the sentences. Select the best answer to complete the sentence.

12. It is difficult to cut costs without _____ quality.
    (A) the sacrifice
    (B) sacrificed
    (C) sacrificing
    (D) sacrificing with   Ⓐ Ⓑ Ⓒ Ⓓ

13. You should not put off _____ the problems.
    (A) dealing with
    (B) deal with
    (C) the deal of
    (D) the dealing of   Ⓐ Ⓑ Ⓒ Ⓓ

14. _____ the customer demand is often very difficult.
    (A) Meeting with
    (B) Meeting to
    (C) To meet
    (D) To be met with   Ⓐ Ⓑ Ⓒ Ⓓ

15. His responsibilities include _____ phones and setting up meetings.
    (A) answered
    (B) to answer
    (C) were answered
    (D) answering   Ⓐ Ⓑ Ⓒ Ⓓ

Read the text that follows. A word, phrase, or sentence is missing in parts of the text. Select the best answer to complete the text.

Questions 16 - 19 refer to the following memo.

To: TriBond Product Development Team
From: Melissa Nguyen
Date: January 21, 2020
Subject: Product Testing

Dear Team Members,

I am happy to inform you that we are ready to _____ our new high-strength
                                                              16.
glue, TriBond. It is good for building plastic models of cars and robots. I would like

to ask each of you to take _____ a sample of TriBond and some kits of plastic
                                        17.
models, and _____ it with our previous glue.
                   18.
We would like to discuss the differences between the new glue and the previous

one at the next meeting. _____.
                                  19.

Melissa Nguyen
TriBond Product Manager

---

16. (A) launch   (B) lead

　　　 (C) load   (D) lean

Ⓐ Ⓑ Ⓒ Ⓓ

17. (A) to home   (B) at home

　　　 (C) in home   (D) home

Ⓐ Ⓑ Ⓒ Ⓓ

18. (A) finish   (B) start

　　　 (C) compare   (D) recommend

Ⓐ Ⓑ Ⓒ Ⓓ

19. (A) Our guest speaker is to make a presentation on the policy.

　　　 (B) Please give me back the sample as soon as possible.

　　　 (C) I am looking forward to your findings and opinions.

　　　 (D) Thank you very much for your advice.

Ⓐ Ⓑ Ⓒ Ⓓ

Read the following text. Select the best answer for each question.

Questions 20 - 22 refer to the following article.

REACTOZ Responds to Falling Sales

—[1]— REACTOZ Computer Games reported an unexpected sales decline for its classic "Zombie Invasion" game during the first three quarters of this year. —[2]— The company aims to increase sales by selling a follow-up version of their previously popular title, titled "Revenge of the Zombie Invasion."

—[3]— By doing so, the company said it hopes to keep those customers interested in its products and expand its market share. —[4]—

---

20. **How long have the sales been declining?**
(A) Three months
(B) Six months
(C) Nine months
(D) One year
    Ⓐ Ⓑ Ⓒ Ⓓ

21. **How does REACTOZ plan to increase sales?**
(A) By creating entirely new games
(B) By creating a follow-up version
(C) By responding to consumer requests
(D) By working with other game companies
    Ⓐ Ⓑ Ⓒ Ⓓ

22. **In which of the positions marked [1], [2], [3], and [4] does the following sentence best belong?**
"This version of the game will feature new characters and enhanced, attractive themes."
(A) [1]
(B) [2]
(C) [3]
(D) [4]

11 Traffic

🎧 Listening Section

🔥 *Before Listening*

☑ Vocabulary check

Choose the correct meaning for each word or phrase.

1. downtown	(	)	**2.** give ~ a ride	(	)
3. occupation	(	)	**4.** reduce	(	)
5. speeding	(	)	**6.** traffic accident	(	)
7. traffic jam	(	)	**8.** update	(	)

スピード違反	繁華街	減らす	交通渋滞
交通事故	職業	（人を）車に乗せる	最新情報

🎧42 Part **1** Photographs

You will hear four statements about a picture. Select the one statement that best describes what you see in the picture.

1.

Ⓐ Ⓑ Ⓒ Ⓓ

2.

Ⓐ Ⓑ Ⓒ Ⓓ

Part 2 Question-Response

You will hear a question or statement and three responses. Select the best response to the question or statement.

3. Mark your answer on your answer sheet.   Ⓐ Ⓑ Ⓒ

4. Mark your answer on your answer sheet.   Ⓐ Ⓑ Ⓒ

5. Mark your answer on your answer sheet.   Ⓐ Ⓑ Ⓒ

Part 3 Conversation

You will hear a conversation between two or more people. You will be asked to answer three questions about what the speakers say in the conversation. Select the best response to each question.

6. **What is the man's occupation?**
   (A) Police officer
   (B) Truck driver
   (C) Firefighter
   (D) Ticket agent   Ⓐ Ⓑ Ⓒ Ⓓ

7. **Why was the woman stopped?**
   (A) She drove too slowly.
   (B) She was in a no-parking zone.
   (C) She was speeding.
   (D) She has no free ticket.   Ⓐ Ⓑ Ⓒ Ⓓ

8. **What does the woman receive from the man?**
   (A) A driver's license
   (B) A travel pass
   (C) A discount coupon
   (D) A speeding ticket   Ⓐ Ⓑ Ⓒ Ⓓ

TOEIC®

11

Traffic

You will hear a talk given by a single speaker. You will be asked to answer three questions about what the speaker says in the talk. Select the best response to each question.

9. **Why was Parkland Drive reduced to one lane?**
   (A) The road was under construction.
   (B) The bridge was damaged.
   (C) There was a car accident.
   (D) There was heavy snow.

   (A) (B) (C) (D)

10. **Where can drivers expect the traffic jam to be?**
    (A) Parkland Drive
    (B) Washington Driveway
    (C) Main Street
    (D) Emerson Avenue

    (A) (B) (C) (D)

11. **When will the traffic news be updated?**
    (A) In 13 minutes
    (B) In 30 minutes
    (C) In one hour
    (D) Tomorrow morning

    (A) (B) (C) (D)

📖 Reading Section

✒ *Before Reading*

☑ Vocabulary check

Choose the correct meaning for each word or phrase.

1. agenda	(	)	**2.** board member	(	)	
3. newcomer	(	)	**4.** punish	(	)	
5. reminder	(	)	**6.** retire	(	)	
7. inspect	(	)	**8.** mechanic	(	)	

役員	議題	新人	辞める
検査する	罰する	催促状	機械工

84

■ 助動詞 ■

助動詞とは、動詞に意味を付け加える働きをする言葉で、can（〜することができる）、must（〜しなければならない）、may（〜かもしれない）等が挙げられます。1つの助動詞にはたいてい2つ以上の意味があります。助動詞は動詞の前に置かれ、後に続く動詞は原形になります。

●助動詞がある文の語順

肯定文	He can speak English.（彼は英語を話すことができます。） 主語＋助動詞＋動詞の原形
否定文	He cannot (can't) speak English.（彼は英語を話すことができません。） 主語＋助動詞＋ not ＋動詞の原形
疑問文	Can he speak English?（彼は英語を話すことができますか。） 助動詞＋主語＋動詞の原形

●重要な助動詞とその意味

can	〜することができる 〜する可能性がある
could	〜することができる（ありうる）だろう 〜することができた
will	〜するつもりである 〜することになる
would	〜であろう 〜したものだった
may	〜かもしれない 〜してもよい
might	〜かもしれない（mayより控えめな表現） 〜することもありうるだろう
must	〜しなければならない 〜にちがいない
shall	Shall I …?（私が〜しましょうか） Shall we …?（一緒に〜しましょうか）
should	〜すべきである 〜するはずだ

（例）He may not come back to the office.

（彼はオフィスに戻らないかもしれません。）

You must be busy at this time of the year.

（毎年この時期あなたは忙しいに違いありません。）

Choose the correct word to complete each sentence.

(1) All the newcomers should _____ the orientation session next Friday.

    (A) attends   (B) attend   (A) (B)

(2) _____ I see your passport?

    (A) Must   (B) May   (A) (B)

Part 5 Incomplete Sentences

A word or phrase is missing in each of the sentences. Select the best answer to complete the sentence.

12. Mr. Wong and the local sales staff _____ attend the seminar from 2 p.m.
    (A) must have
    (B) will have
    (C) must
    (D) shall be   (A) (B) (C) (D)

13. All the board members _____ take 10 extra days off during the summer.
    (A) can
    (B) would have
    (C) could be
    (D) will be   (A) (B) (C) (D)

14. Laffin Tech's CEO Dan Rowan announced that he _____ next month.
    (A) is retire
    (B) would retire
    (C) retired
    (D) had retired   (A) (B) (C) (D)

15. _____ we move on to the next agenda item?
    (A) May
    (B) Have
    (C) Shall
    (D) Might   (A) (B) (C) (D)

Read the text that follows. A word, phrase, or sentence is missing in parts of the text. Select the best answer to complete the text.

Questions 16 - 19 refer to the following notice.

Reminder: Regular Inspection for Your Car is an Absolute Must

You must have your car _____, or you may be punished with a fine. Without

16.
an inspection sticker, you may be fined _____ to $500, even if nothing

17.
seems _____ with the car. For your car inspection, you should go to any

18.
automobile mechanic shop. _____.

19.

---

16. (A) inspect
    (B) inspecting
    (C) inspected
    (D) inspection
    (A) (B) (C) (D)

17. (A) up
    (B) on
    (C) as
    (D) by
    (A) (B) (C) (D)

18. (A) good
    (B) fine
    (C) mistake
    (D) wrong
    (A) (B) (C) (D)

19. (A) For information on your nearest mechanic shop, please check our website.
    (B) To get a new sticker, visit our website immediately.
    (C) Please remove your car now or you'll be fined.
    (D) You must check the condition of your car by yourself.
    (A) (B) (C) (D)

11

TOEIC®

Traffic

Read the following text. Select the best answer for each question.

Question 20 - 22 refer to the following text message.

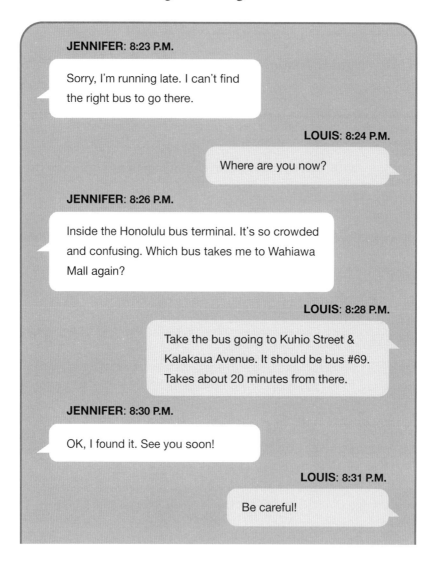

JENNIFER: 8:23 P.M.

Sorry, I'm running late. I can't find the right bus to go there.

LOUIS: 8:24 P.M.

Where are you now?

JENNIFER: 8:26 P.M.

Inside the Honolulu bus terminal. It's so crowded and confusing. Which bus takes me to Wahiawa Mall again?

LOUIS: 8:28 P.M.

Take the bus going to Kuhio Street & Kalakaua Avenue. It should be bus #69. Takes about 20 minutes from there.

JENNIFER: 8:30 P.M.

OK, I found it. See you soon!

LOUIS: 8:31 P.M.

Be careful!

20. **Why is Jennifer late for the meeting?**
   (A) She was caught in a traffic jam.
   (B) She was involved in a car accident.
   (C) She took the wrong bus.
   (D) She forgot which bus to take.

21. **Where will they meet?**

    (A) At the Honolulu bus terminal

    (B) At a concert hall

    (C) At Wahiawa Mall

    (D) At Waikiki Beach   Ⓐ Ⓑ Ⓒ Ⓓ

22. **At 8:31 P.M., what does Louis likely mean when he writes, "Be careful"?**

    (A) Do not take a wrong bus.

    (B) Take care on your way.

    (C) Make sure you will not be late again.

    (D) Drive carefully.   Ⓐ Ⓑ Ⓒ Ⓓ

Unit

12 Finance and Banking

Listening Section

Before Listening

☑ Vocabulary check

Choose the correct meaning for each word or phrase.

1. bank account   (   )   2. complain   (   )
3. hold   (   )   4. out of order   (   )
5. representative   (   )   6. save money   (   )
7. savings account   (   )   8. withdraw   (   )

貯金する	銀行口座	苦情を言う	故障中で
担当者	電話を切らずに待つ	（預金を）引き出す	普通預金口座

Part 1 Photographs

You will hear four statements about a picture. Select the one statement that best describes what you see in the picture.

1.

Ⓐ Ⓑ Ⓒ Ⓓ

2.

Ⓐ Ⓑ Ⓒ Ⓓ

Part 2 Question-Response

You will hear a question or statement and three responses. Select the best response to the question or statement.

3. Mark your answer on your answer sheet. Ⓐ Ⓑ Ⓒ

4. Mark your answer on your answer sheet. Ⓐ Ⓑ Ⓒ

5. Mark your answer on your answer sheet. Ⓐ Ⓑ Ⓒ

Part 3 Conversation

You will hear a conversation between two or more people. You will be asked to answer three questions about what the speakers say in the conversation. Select the best response to each question.

6. **Where are the speakers?**
   (A) At a station
   (B) At an office
   (C) At a ticket gate
   (D) At a bank Ⓐ Ⓑ Ⓒ Ⓓ

7. **What does the man want to do?**
   (A) Transfer some money
   (B) Withdraw some money
   (C) Fix the ATM
   (D) Work at a bank Ⓐ Ⓑ Ⓒ Ⓓ

8. **What does the woman suggest the man do?**
   (A) Get a new ATM
   (B) Go to a different bank
   (C) Use a different ATM
   (D) Close the bank account Ⓐ Ⓑ Ⓒ Ⓓ

You will hear a talk given by a single speaker. You will be asked to answer three questions about what the speaker says in the talk. Select the best response to each question.

9. **Who is probably the speaker?**
    (A) An accountant
    (B) A bank clerk
    (C) A sales representative
    (D) A customer service representative   (A)(B)(C)(D)

10. **What number should the caller push to complain about the company's service?**
    (A) 1
    (B) 2
    (C) 3
    (D) 4   (A)(B)(C)(D)

11. **What does the recorded voice mean when it says, "One of our representatives will be with you in a moment"?**
    (A) A service representative will answer the call before long.
    (B) A service representative will visit the caller soon.
    (C) A sales manager will solve the problem immediately.
    (D) A telephone operator will hang up the phone.   (A)(B)(C)(D)

📖 Reading Section

🖋 *Before Reading*

☑ Vocabulary check

Choose the correct meaning for each word or phrase.

1. amount ( )	2. branch ( )
3. earn ( )	4. guarantee ( )
5. invest ( )	6. register ( )
7. stock market ( )	8. transfer ( )

登録する	投資する	支店	額
稼ぐ	送金する	保証する	株式市場

■ 前置詞 ■

前置詞は、名詞もしくは動名詞の前に置かれ、場所や時、状態等を表します。前置詞には、in , on, at, of, for 等があり、文中では以下の例のように使われます。

（例）　He lives **in** New York.（彼はニューヨークに住んでいます。）

　　　The musical lasts **for** three hours.（ミュージカルは3時間続きます。）

　　　I'm good **at** cooking.（私は料理が上手です。）

　　場所や時を表す前置詞を使う場合、以下のような規則を覚えておくと役立ちます。

	in	on	at
場所	in Tokyo	on Takeshita Street	at the café
時間	in 1990	on December 24th	at 5 p.m.
	in December	on Mondays	at noon

また、以下のように2つ以上の語句が結合し、前置詞の役割を持つもの（前置詞句）もあります。これ以外にもたくさんの前置詞句がありますので、その都度覚えていくよう心がけましょう。

according to （～ によれば）	apart from （～は別として）
as for （～に関しては)	because of （～のために）
due to （～のために）	except for （～を除いては）
instead of （～の代わりに）	in order to （～するために）
on behalf of （～の代表として）	owing to （～ のために）
regardless of （～にもかかわらず）	up to （～ まで）

（例題）　I would like to thank all employees ＿＿＿＿＿＿ their hard work.

　　　　(A) to　　　(B) with　　　(C) by　　　(D) for

（解答）　(D) for （従業員全員にその懸命な働きぶりに対して私はお礼を申し上げたいと
　　　　思います。）

　　　　「thank 人＋ for」で「人に～に対してお礼を言う」という意味になるので正解は
　　　　(D) になります。

Choose the correct word to complete each sentence.

(1) We will have a meeting tomorrow _____ 2 o'clock.

    (A) at   (B) in   (A) (B)

(2) How many days are there _____ February?

    (A) at   (B) in   (A) (B)

Part 5 Incomplete Sentences

A word or phrase is missing in each of the sentences. Select the best answer to complete the sentence.

12. Janet works _____ Seattle now.

    (A) in

    (B) on

    (C) at

    (D) from   (A) (B) (C) (D)

13. He was late this morning _____ the heavy traffic.

    (A) out of

    (B) across

    (C) along

    (D) because of   (A) (B) (C) (D)

14. According _____ the sales manager, their sales increased last quarter.

    (A) to

    (B) with

    (C) by

    (D) for   (A) (B) (C) (D)

15. _____ order to earn money, Silkwood Community Center holds auctions every Sunday.

    (A) To

    (B) In

    (C) At

    (D) Of   (A) (B) (C) (D)

Read the text that follows. A word, phrase, or sentence is missing in parts of the text. Select the best answer to complete the text.

Questions 16 - 19 refer to the following e-mail.

To: customer-service@firstbank.com
From: Martha Khumalo-Cook <marthakc@personalmail.com>
Subject: Account inquiry

To Whom It May Concern,

My mother transferred $500 into my account on May 30. _____. It shows that
                                                                    16.
the amount is $478, _____ is $22 less. My account number is 0367-2346, with
                         17.
my bank branch _____ Toronto. Please _____ me in this matter.
                      18.   **19.**

Thank you,

Martha Khumalo-Cook

16. (A) I want to know how to deposit money through an ATM.
    (B) I think I have to open a bank account soon.
    (C) I just checked my account on your Internet banking website.
    (D) I closed my account 10 days ago.   Ⓐ Ⓑ Ⓒ Ⓓ

17. (A) who
    (B) which
    (C) whom
    (D) that   Ⓐ Ⓑ Ⓒ Ⓓ

18. (A) on
    (B) at
    (C) in
    (D) for   Ⓐ Ⓑ Ⓒ Ⓓ

19. (A) take
    (B) help
    (C) save
    (D) get   Ⓐ Ⓑ Ⓒ Ⓓ

Read the following texts. Select the best answer for each question.

Questions 20 - 24 refer to the following online notice and form.

The Wise Investors© Online Seminar

If you have never invested on your own, or if you have never invested successfully, our Wise Investors© Online Seminar will teach you very safe and simple ways to make your money.

Starting January 15th, in this three-week online seminar, you will:
- *Learn effective investment plans*
- *Develop your own plan for regular savings*

Best of all, you can learn at home! Click the link below to enroll.
~ 100% money-back satisfaction guaranteed ~
www.wiseinvestors/seminar/signup/go

WELCOME TO THE WISE INVESTORS© ONLINE SEMINAR HOMEPAGE

Please fill out the form below to register for our seminar.

First Name: **BOB**   Last Name: **EUBANKS**
Today's Date: 01/05/2020

Investing Experience: ×   None
                                Little
                                Some
                                A lot

Payment Method: ×   Credit Card
                          Check
                          Online Bank Transfer

Reason for Attending:

I've read some books about investing, but all of them confused me. I think I really need to learn how to invest with the help of someone who knows what to do.

20. **What will participants learn about?**

(A) How to get a bank loan

(B) How to save their pensions

(C) How to navigate the stock market

(D) How to make an investment plan

21. **What is an advantage of this seminar?**

(A) Learning at home

(B) Meeting famous businesspeople

(C) Studying investment for free

(D) Receiving discounts

22. **Who is Bob Eubanks?**

(A) A seminar host

(B) A participant in the seminar

(C) An experienced businessperson

(D) A financial consultant

23. **When can Bob Eubanks join the seminar?**

(A) In two days

(B) In three days

(C) In 10 days

(D) In three weeks

24. **What may happen if Bob Eubanks is not satisfied with the seminar?**

(A) Invest his money

(B) Borrow his money

(C) Lose his money

(D) Get his money back

Unit

13 Media

 Listening Section

🖐 *Before Listening*

☑ **Vocabulary check**

Choose the correct meaning for each word or phrase.

1.	financial	(	)	**2.**	remote control	( )
3.	in no hurry	(	)	**4.**	issue	( )
5.	lay off	(	)	**6.**	official	( )
7.	plumber	(	)	**8.**	real estate agent	( )

不動産業者	職員、当局者	解雇する	急がないで
（定期刊行物の）号	リモコン	財政上の	配管工

🎧 50 **Part 1 Photographs**

You will hear four statements about a picture. Select the one statement that best describes what you see in the picture.

1.

Ⓐ Ⓑ Ⓒ Ⓓ

2.

Ⓐ Ⓑ Ⓒ Ⓓ

Part 2 Question-Response

You will hear a question or statement and three responses. Select the best response to the question or statement.

3. Mark your answer on your answer sheet. (A)(B)(C)

4. Mark your answer on your answer sheet. (A)(B)(C)

5. Mark your answer on your answer sheet. (A)(B)(C)

52 **Part 3** Conversation

You will hear a conversation between two or more people. You will be asked to answer three questions about what the speakers say in the conversation. Select the best response to each question.

6. **What is the man's occupation?**
   (A) Real estate agent
   (B) Repairperson
   (C) Computer programmer
   (D) Plumber (A)(B)(C)(D)

7. **Why does the woman have to wait until Monday?**
   (A) The shop is closed.
   (B) The man has other jobs.
   (C) The woman cannot bring the television.
   (D) There is a major problem with the television. (A)(B)(C)(D)

8. **What does the woman probably do next?**
   (A) She writes down her contact number.
   (B) She goes to another shop.
   (C) She fixes the television.
   (D) She finds another mechanic. (A)(B)(C)(D)

TOEIC®

13

Media

You will hear a talk given by a single speaker. You will be asked to answer three questions about what the speaker says in the talk. Select the best response to each question.

9. **What will North East Airlines probably do?**
   (A) Hire more flight attendants
   (B) Reduce their workers
   (C) Offer better service
   (D) Decrease international flights   Ⓐ Ⓑ Ⓒ Ⓓ

10. **How long has North East Airlines been in financial trouble?**
    (A) One year
    (B) Two years
    (C) Three years
    (D) Four years   Ⓐ Ⓑ Ⓒ Ⓓ

11. **Who is responsible for the decision?**
    (A) The airline workers
    (B) The pilots of North East Airlines
    (C) The airline officials
    (D) The new CEO of North East Airlines   Ⓐ Ⓑ Ⓒ Ⓓ

📖 Reading Section

☝ *Before Reading*

☑ Vocabulary check

Choose the correct meaning for each word or phrase.

1.	browse	(	)	2.	damaged product	(	)
3.	go online	(	)	4.	publication	(	)
5.	rank… as ～	(	)	6.	rapidly	(	)
7.	retailer	(	)	8.	subscription	(	)

刊行物	定期購読	閲覧する	欠陥商品
～を…と位置づける	インターネットに接続する	急速に	小売業者

100

■ 接続詞 ■

接続詞は文と文、あるいは1つの文の中で、語と語、句と句、節と節を結びつける働きをします。例えば、and（そして）、but（しかし）、or（または）、so（だから、それで）、nor（〜もまた…ない）等が挙げられます。

（例） Do you come to work by car **or** by train?
（あなたは車で会社に行きますか、それとも電車で行きますか。）
His colleagues take on his work **while** he is away from the office.
（彼がオフィスを離れている間、同僚たちが彼の仕事を引き受けます。）

その他にも、次の表に挙げる接続詞は特に重要なので覚えるようにしてください。

時		原因		条件		譲歩	
when	（〜する時）	because	（〜だから）	if	（もし〜ならば）	though	（〜だけれども）
as	（〜の時に、しながら）	since	（〜だから）	unless	（もし〜しなければ）	although	（〜だけれども）
while	（〜している間に）	as	（〜だから）			even if	（たとえ〜でも）
since	（〜以来）					even though	（たとえ〜でも）
after	（〜してから）						
as soon as	（〜するとすぐに）						

（例題） My boss not only gave me a good evaluation, ＿＿＿＿＿ allowed me to take 10 days off.
(A) so　　(B) but also　　(C) while　　(D) though

（解答）(B) but also（私の上司は私に良い評価をくれただけでなく、10日間の休暇を取ることを許可してくれました。）
not only … but also 〜（…だけでなく、〜も）はよく TOEIC® L&R Test に出題されます。

● 命令文＋and / or
（例） Get up early, and you will catch the train.
（早く起きなさい、そうすれば電車に間に合いますよ。）
命令文の後ろにandが続くと、「〜しなさい、そうすれば…」という意味になります。
（例） Hurry up, or you will be late.
（急ぎなさい、そうしないと遅れますよ。）
命令文の後ろにorが続くと、「〜しなさい、そうしなければ…」という意味になります。

TOEIC®

13

Media

Choose the correct word to complete each sentence.

(1) The seminar was informative for both staff _____ engineers.

(A) and   (B) or   Ⓐ Ⓑ

(2) _____ you want to start a business by yourself, you should save a lot of money.

(A) Although   (B) If   Ⓐ Ⓑ

Part 5 Incomplete Sentences

A word or phrase is missing in each of the sentences. Select the best answer to complete the sentence.

12. _____ the old office manager left, the CEO hired Ms. Morgan.

(A) Unless

(B) Therefore

(C) However

(D) When   Ⓐ Ⓑ Ⓒ Ⓓ

13. Your order will be processed _____ sent within 24 hours.

(A) and

(B) but

(C) or

(D) so   Ⓐ Ⓑ Ⓒ Ⓓ

14. The marketing staff members looked very tired _____ they had to work until 10 p.m.

(A) though

(B) after

(C) so

(D) because   Ⓐ Ⓑ Ⓒ Ⓓ

15. Neither the factory _____ the retailers are responsible for the damaged products.

(A) or

(B) and

(C) nor

(D) but   Ⓐ Ⓑ Ⓒ Ⓓ

Read the text that follows. A word, phrase, or sentence is missing in parts of the text. Select the best answer to complete the text.

Questions 16 - 19 refer to the following advertisement.

The Magazine Bazaar Website

Do you like magazines? If so, _____ out the Magazine Bazaar website. We offer
                                            16.
magazine subscriptions to an _____ wide variety of publications. _____.
                                    17.   **18.**
Then, the catalogue will be sent to you _____ mail. You can also go online and
                                                19.
browse our whole catalog on the Web!

---

16. (A) click
    (B) see
    (C) kick
    (D) check   Ⓐ Ⓑ Ⓒ Ⓓ

17. (A) incredible
    (B) incredibly
    (C) incredibleness
    (D) incredulity   Ⓐ Ⓑ Ⓒ Ⓓ

18. (A) We would like to offer a large discount to our members.
    (B) Thank you very much for your order.
    (C) First, please download the online magazines.
    (D) Please request a free hard copy of our catalog today.   Ⓐ Ⓑ Ⓒ Ⓓ

19. (A) through
    (B) with
    (C) by
    (D) for   Ⓐ Ⓑ Ⓒ Ⓓ

TOEIC®

13

Media

Read the following texts. Select the best answer for each question.

Question 20 - 24 refer to the following advertisement, plan, and form.

Let **MUSIC PALACE** Take You There

Welcome to MUSIC PALACE — the future of digital music streaming.

LP records and cassette tapes are a thing of the distant past, and CDs too are rapidly disappearing. Online streaming is the future of music listening — and MUSIC PALACE is proud to be the No. 1 streaming choice of music lovers everywhere.

With more than 20 million songs in our extensive catalog to listen to and several affordable plans to choose from, it is no wonder that *MuzikFan* magazine ranks MUSIC PALACE as "the biggest, the best, the most awesome online music streaming source" in the world. That's an accomplishment we are very proud of.

Listening to all the music you love, anywhere and at any time, is like taking a journey to a magical, digital place. Let MUSIC PALACE be the online streaming source that takes you there.

To get started right away, click here to choose one of our flexible, affordable MUSIC PALACE plans and open a new account. Your favorite music awaits you!

Choose Your Plan

Choose Your **MUSIC PALACE** Plan

Play millions of songs ad-free, on-demand and offline — anytime, anywhere.
Enjoy high-quality digital sound on all of your devices!

Pick your Plan...

— Individual Plan —
$10 per month
· Listen to music ad-free
· Play anywhere (even offline)
· Play on-demand
· Play any song even on mobile

— Family Plan —
$20 per month
· 6 accounts for family members living under one roof
· Make a playlist for your family
· Regularly uploaded music enjoyed by all
· Ad-free music listening
· Play offline & on-demand
· Play any song even on mobile

— Student Plan —
$5 per month
· Ad-supported music plan
· Play anywhere (even offline)
· Play on-demand
· Play any song even on mobile

Make Your Payment

TOEIC®

13

Media

Make Your **MUSIC PALACE** Payment

Enter all the information fields, then click on the Pay Now button below:

First Name: Ricky **Last Name:** Ricardo

E-mail: ricky-babalu@mail.com

Plan: Student

Date of subscription: 22 December 2019

I wish to pay by:

☒ Credit card   ☐ Bank transfer   ☐ PayEasy

Comments:

I've read your advertisement, but I have some questions. You have 20 million songs in the music library, but can I also access whole albums or free music videos? I don't have any mobile devices. Is Music Palace available on a desktop computer too?

PAY NOW

---

20. **What do subscribers get by signing up for the Music Palace service?**

(A) Home stereo accessories

(B) Rare and used CDs

(C) Internet music streaming

(D) Online gaming networks

Ⓐ Ⓑ Ⓒ Ⓓ

21. **What kind of service does Music Palace NOT offer?**
    (A) Listening to music on all computer devices
    (B) Accessing to music offline
    (C) Playing music from its catalog
    (D) Free musical instrument lessons

22. **In the advertisement, the word "extensive" in paragraph 3, line 1, is closest in meaning to:**
    (A) large
    (B) heavy
    (C) small
    (D) limited

23. **What is said about the family plan?**
    (A) It is the cheapest plan of the three.
    (B) Music is interrupted by advertisements.
    (C) Six people can use it if they live together.
    (D) Each family member has his/her own playlist.

24. **What is indicated about Mr. Ricardo?**
    (A) He owns a lot of music albums.
    (B) He wants to listen to music on a home computer.
    (C) He likes only certain kinds of music.
    (D) He does not have a student ID.

14 Health and Welfare

🎧 Listening Section

👆 *Before Listening*

☑ Vocabulary check

Choose the correct meaning for each word or phrase.

1. dental clinic	(	)	**2.** exercise	(	)
3. hold on to	(	)	**4.** make time for	(	)
5. medicine	(	)	**6.** receptionist	(	)
7. register	(	)	**8.** suffer from	(	)

〜をつかんで離さない	歯科	〜のために時間を作る	〜を患う
登録する	受付係	薬	運動

🎧 54 **Part 1 Photographs**

You will hear four statements about a picture. Select the one statement that best describes what you see in the picture.

1.

Ⓐ Ⓑ Ⓒ Ⓓ

2.

Ⓐ Ⓑ Ⓒ Ⓓ

You will hear a question or statement and three responses. Select the best response to the question or statement.

3. Mark your answer on your answer sheet. Ⓐ Ⓑ Ⓒ

4. Mark your answer on your answer sheet. Ⓐ Ⓑ Ⓒ

5. Mark your answer on your answer sheet. Ⓐ Ⓑ Ⓒ

🎧 56 | **Part 3** Conversation

You will hear a conversation between two or more people. You will be asked to answer three questions about what the speakers say in the conversation. Select the best response to each question.

6. **What does the woman's doctor recommend?**
    (A) Get enough sleep
    (B) Take a rest
    (C) Get up early in the morning
    (D) Do some exercise Ⓐ Ⓑ Ⓒ Ⓓ

7. **What are the speakers about to do?**
    (A) Work together
    (B) Take a walk together
    (C) Take a dog outside
    (D) Work at home Ⓐ Ⓑ Ⓒ Ⓓ

8. **Why does the woman get up early?**
    (A) To start work earlier than usual
    (B) To study with the man
    (C) To make lunch for the man
    (D) To follow the doctor's advice Ⓐ Ⓑ Ⓒ Ⓓ

TOEIC®

14

Health and Welfare

You will hear a talk given by a single speaker. You will be asked to answer three questions about what the speaker says in the talk. Select the best response to each question.

9. **What is the main purpose of the announcement?**
   (A) A new computer system for membership cards
   (B) The company's financial problems
   (C) New staff members being hired
   (D) Repairs to the gym machines   Ⓐ Ⓑ Ⓒ Ⓓ

10. **What will the members probably do at the sports club?**
    (A) Check the admission fee of the sports club
    (B) Throw away their membership card at the front desk
    (C) Check the availability of new machines
    (D) Register their fingerprint   Ⓐ Ⓑ Ⓒ Ⓓ

11. **Look at the chart. What do customers have to do to enter the club on Sunday, after March 20?**
    (A) Call the receptionists
    (B) Use the new computer system
    (C) Show their membership card to one of the receptionists
    (D) Leave their membership card at home   Ⓐ Ⓑ Ⓒ Ⓓ

Receptionists' Availability: ○ *on duty* × *off duty*		
	8:00 a.m. – 7:00 p.m.	7:00 p.m. – 10:00 p.m
Monday thru Friday	○	×
Saturday and Sunday	×	×

📖 Reading Section

🎋 *Before Reading*

☑ Vocabulary check

Choose the correct meaning for each word or phrase.

1.	extension	( )		2.	facility	( )
3.	field	( )		4.	free of charge	( )
5.	notify	( )		6.	job postings	( )
7.	search for	( )		8.	take advantage of	( )

無料で	〜を利用する	施設	分野
知らせる	内線	〜を探す	求人

■ 比較 ■

●原級

as ＋形容詞・副詞の原級 ＋ as「〜は〜と同じくらい…だ」

Your room is **as big as** mine.（あなたの部屋は私の部屋と同じくらい大きいです。）

●比較級

比較級 ＋ than「〜より…だ」

Your room is bigg**er than** mine.（あなたの部屋は私のよりも大きいです。）

●最上級

the ＋最上級 ＋ of (in)「〜の中で最も…だ」

Your room is **the** bigg**est of** all.（あなたの部屋はすべての中で一番大きいです。）

●原級（元の形のままの形容詞、または副詞）を比較級、最上級に変化させるときの規則

	原級	比較級	最上級
【1音節と2音節の1部の単語】			
意味	（そのまま）	より、もっと	一番、最も
安い	cheap	cheaper	cheapest
古い	old	older	oldest
【2音節以上のほとんどの単語】			
有名な	famous	more famous	most famous
急速に	rapidly	more rapidly	most rapidly
着実に	steadily	more steadily	most steadily
【不規則変化】			
良い / 健康な	good / well	better	best
悪い / 病気の	bad / ill	worse	worst
多数の / 多量の	many / much	more	most
少しの	little	less	least

（例題） This manual is as ＿＿＿＿＿＿＿＿ as that manual.

(A) useful　　(B) more useful　　(C) usefulness　　(D) most useful

（解答） (A) useful（この説明書はあの説明書と同じくらい使い勝手が良いです。）
「〜は〜と同じくらい…だ」と表現したいときには as と as の間に原級を入れます。したがって、原級の (A) が正解になります。

TOEIC®

14

Health and Welfare

Choose the correct word to complete each sentence.

(1) Your office is _____ than our office.

   (A) large   (B) larger   Ⓐ Ⓑ

(2) Our branch manager speaks French the _____ in the company.

   (A) more fluently   (B) most fluently   Ⓐ Ⓑ

Part 5 Incomplete Sentences

A word or phrase is missing in each of the sentences. Select the best answer to complete the sentence.

12. You are the _____ person I know.

   (A) busier

   (B) busiest

   (C) more busy

   (D) most busy   Ⓐ Ⓑ Ⓒ Ⓓ

13. Our company is _____ in the field.

   (A) the most competitive

   (B) more competitive

   (C) competition

   (D) competitive   Ⓐ Ⓑ Ⓒ Ⓓ

14. This brochure is _____ than the old one.

   (A) more attractively

   (B) attraction

   (C) the most attractive

   (D) more attractive   Ⓐ Ⓑ Ⓒ Ⓓ

15. Online job postings allow you to search for a new job much more _____ .

   (A) easier

   (B) easy

   (C) easiest

   (D) easily   Ⓐ Ⓑ Ⓒ Ⓓ

Read the text that follows. A word, phrase, or sentence is missing in parts of the text. Select the best answer to complete the text.

Questions 16 - 19 refer to the following letter.

Jason Chopra III
113 Regent Street,
Austin, Texas 78703

Dear Mr. Chopra,

You have requested an _____ with the eye specialist at our clinic, Dr. Williams.
                        16.
However, he is on vacation right now. _____. If you would like to _____
                                        17.   **18.**
another doctor, please call us at 331-5598. However, if you would prefer to see Dr.

Williams, we will be sure to notify you as soon as he _____ back.
                                                        19.

---

16. (A) appliance
    (B) application
    (C) appearance
    (D) appointment
    Ⓐ Ⓑ Ⓒ Ⓓ

17. (A) He will be returning by the end of next week.
    (B) He's leaving soon, so you should find a new doctor.
    (C) We apologize for the late delivery.
    (D) We are sorry, but we have only one eye specialist.
    Ⓐ Ⓑ Ⓒ Ⓓ

18. (A) see
    (B) go
    (C) operate
    (D) suffer
    Ⓐ Ⓑ Ⓒ Ⓓ

19. (A) get
    (B) gets
    (C) will get
    (D) is going to get
    Ⓐ Ⓑ Ⓒ Ⓓ

Read the following text. Select the best answer for each question.

Questions 20 - 22 refer to the following e-mail.

TO: All Edisent Energy Co. Employees

FROM: Samantha Lucci

SUBJECT: Employee Fitness Facility

The Edisent Employee Fitness Facility is now complete. All employees of Edisent Energy Co. may take advantage of the facility.

The fitness equipment includes four treadmills, two bicycles, two stretch machines, and strength-training machines. A locker room with showers and storage is also available. Towels will be provided free of charge.

Facility hours will run from 6:00 a.m. to 8:00 p.m. Monday through Friday. John Shaft will act as the facilities manager. Please contact him at extension #971 if you have any questions.

Samantha Lucci
Employee Benefits Coordinator

---

20. **What does the e-mail tell employees?**
   (A) New training machines have been added.
   (B) Facility hours have changed.
   (C) The Employee Fitness Facility will open.
   (D) The Employee Fitness Facility will close.

21. **What will be offered at the fitness facility?**
   (A) Pay phones
   (B) A sauna
   (C) Use on holidays
   (D) Training machines

   Ⓐ Ⓑ Ⓒ Ⓓ

22. **How do employees contact John Shaft?**

(A) By writing an office memo

(B) By calling on the office phone

(C) By visiting his office

(D) By sending e-mail

Vocabulary Check List

※日本語の意味の後に記載されている ( ) 内の "L" は LISTENING PART "R" は READING PART を意味します。数字はパートの番号を示しています。各章の Grammar と Practice のセクションに出てきた重要単語も本リストに含まれています。

Unit 1　Eating Out

- [ ] **accountant**【名】会計士 (Grammar)
- [ ] **advertise**【動】宣伝する (L4)
- [ ] **assignment**【名】課題、業務 (L2)
- [ ] **benefit**【名】給付金、福利厚生 (R1)
- [ ] **branch**【名】支店 (Grammar)
- [ ] **cancel**【動】キャンセルする (L4)
- [ ] **co-worker**【名】同僚 (L4)
- [ ] **condition**【名】状況 (Practice)
- [ ] **daily**【形】毎日の (R3)
- [ ] **drink**【名】飲み物 (L4)
- [ ] **empty**【形】空いている (L1)
- [ ] **financial**【形】財政的な (Practice)
- [ ] **free**【形】無料の (R1)
- [ ] **free repair service**
      【名】無料修理サービス (R1)
- [ ] **law**【名】法律 (R1)
- [ ] **lawyer**【名】弁護士 (R1)
- [ ] **make a reservation**【動】予約をす（L4）
- [ ] **marketing**【名】市場、マーケティング (R1)
- [ ] **mention**【動】言及する (R3)
- [ ] **offer**【動】提供する (R1)
- [ ] **order**【動】注文する (L4)
- [ ] **pension**【名】年金 (R1)
- [ ] **policy**【名】方針 (R1)
- [ ] **remind**【名】再確認する (L4)
- [ ] **renovation**【名】改装 (R2)
- [ ] **research**【名】調査 (R1)
- [ ] **reservation**【名】予約 (L4)
- [ ] **rest**【名】残り (R2)
- [ ] **reopen**【動】再オープンする (R2)
- [ ] **sales manager**【名】営業部長 (Grammar)
- [ ] **serve**【動】給仕する、食事などを出す (L2)
- [ ] **supervisor**【名】監督者 (Practice)
- [ ] **take place**【動】行われる (III)
- [ ] **thru (=through)**【前】～の間に (R3)

Unit 2　Travel

- [ ] **according to**～によれば (R1)
- [ ] **achieve**【動】成し遂げる (R1)
- [ ] **aisle seat**【名】通路側の席 (L2)
- [ ] **announce**【動】報告する (L4)
- [ ] **apologize**【動】謝罪する (L4)
- [ ] **available**【形】利用可能な (R2)
- [ ] **be delayed**【動】遅れる (L3)
- [ ] **charge**【名】料金 (R3)
- [ ] **client**【名】顧客 (Grammar)
- [ ] **cost reduction**【名】経費削減 (R1)
- [ ] **delay**【動】遅らせる (L3)
- [ ] **due to**～が原因で、～によって (L4)
- [ ] **financially**【副】財政的に (R1)
- [ ] **flight**【名】フライト、便 （L2, L4)
- [ ] **full**【形】満席の (R2)
- [ ] **guest**【名】客 (R3)
- [ ] **half-day**【形】半日の (R2)
- [ ] **hold**【動】持つ (I)
- [ ] **inconvenience**【名】不便 (L4)
- [ ] **interview**【名】面接 (Practice)
- [ ] **inquiry**【名】問い合わせ (R2)
- [ ] **mechanical**【形】機械の (L4)
- [ ] **pack**【動】詰め込む (L1)
- [ ] **passenger**【名】乗客 (L4)
- [ ] **presentation**【名】発表 (Practice)
- [ ] **product**【名】製品 (R1)
- [ ] **provide**【動】提供する (R1)
- [ ] **recheck**【動】再確認する (L3)
- [ ] **remarkable**【形】目覚ましい (R1)
- [ ] **round-trip**【形】往復の、周遊の (L2)
- [ ] **stay**【名】滞在 (R3)
- [ ] **strike**【名】ストライキ (L4)
- [ ] **struggle**【動】四苦八苦する (R1)
- [ ] **tax**【名】税金 (R3)
- [ ] **thunderstorm**【名】雷雨 (L4)
- [ ] **timetable**【名】時刻表 (L3)
- [ ] **toll-free**【副】フリーダイアルで (R3)
- [ ] **travel agency**【名】旅行社 (L3)
- [ ] **vice president**【名】副社長 (R1)
- [ ] **work experience**【名】職歴 (Practice)

Unit 3 　Amusement

- [ ] **awfully**【副】ひどく、恐ろしく (Grammar)
- [ ] **attraction**【名】呼び物、アトラクション (L4)
- [ ] **be related to**【動】〜と関係している (Practice)
- [ ] **decorate**【動】飾る (Grammar)
- [ ] **discuss**【動】話し合う (L3)
- [ ] **driver's license**【名】運転免許証 (R1)
- [ ] **exhibition**【名】展示 (R2)
- [ ] **final**【形】最後の (L2)
- [ ] **get together**【動】集まる (L3)
- [ ] **giraffe**【名】キリン (L4)
- [ ] **hold**【動】開催する (L2)
- [ ] **ID**【名】身分証明書 (R1)
- [ ] **information**【名】情報 (R3)
- [ ] **instead**【副】その代わりに (L4)
- [ ] **join**【動】参加する (L3)
- [ ] **local**【形】地方の (R3)
- [ ] **miss**【動】逃がす (Grammar)
- [ ] **package**【名】小包 (Practice)
- [ ] **place**【名】場所 (L3)
- [ ] **project**【名】企画 (Practice)
- [ ] **public transportation**
     【名】公共交通機関 (R1)
- [ ] **repeat**【動】繰り返す (R3)
- [ ] **ride**【動】乗り物などに）乗る (L1)
- [ ] **shipping cost**【名】配送料、送料 (Practice)
- [ ] **small and medium-sized business**
     【名】中小企業 (R1)
- [ ] **transportation**【名】交通機関 (R1)
- [ ] **unfortunately**【副】不運にも (Grammar)
- [ ] **valid**【形】有効な (R1)
- [ ] **view**【動】見る (L4)
- [ ] **viewer**【名】視聴者 (R3)
- [ ] **weight**【名】重さ (Practice)
- [ ] **work overtime**【動】残業をする (Grammar)
- [ ] **zoo**【名】動物園 (L4)

Unit 4 　Meetings

- [ ] **agreement**【名】合意 (R1)
- [ ] **attend**【動】出席する (L2, L4, R1)
- [ ] **book**【動】予約する (R3)
- [ ] **brief**【形】短い (R3)
- [ ] **budget**【名】予算、【形】予算に関する (Practice)
- [ ] **condition**【名】状態、状況 (L3)
- [ ] **conference room**【名】会議室 (L2, R3)
- [ ] **contact**【動】連絡を取る (R1)
- [ ] **date**【名】日付 (R3)
- [ ] **discuss**【動】議論する (L1, R3)
- [ ] **employee**【名】従業員 (Practice)
- [ ] **enter**【動】入る (Grammar)
- [ ] **executive**【名】幹部、重役 (R1)
- [ ] **favorable**【形】好ましい (L3)
- [ ] **heavy traffic**【名】交通渋滞 (L3)
- [ ] **honest**【形】ごまかしのない、率直な (L3)
- [ ] **lunch break**【名】昼食休憩 (L3)
- [ ] **manager**【名】経営者 (L3)
- [ ] **marketing campaign**
     【名】販促キャンペーン (L2)
- [ ] **monthly**【形】月の、月例の (L2)
- [ ] **organizing committee**【名】組織委員会 (L3)
- [ ] **politics**【名】政治学 (L3)
- [ ] **postpone**【動】延期する (L2)
- [ ] **price**【名】値段 (Grammar)
- [ ] **quarter**【名】四半期 (R1)
- [ ] **raise**【動】育てる (Grammar)
- [ ] **reach**【動】達する (Grammar)
- [ ] **reserve**【動】予約する、取っておく (R3)
- [ ] **reschedule**【動】予定変更をする (L4)
- [ ] **sales figures**【名】売上高、販売数量 (R1)
- [ ] **sales promotion**【名】販売促進 (R3)
- [ ] **sharply**【副】急激に (Grammar)
- [ ] **strategy**【名】戦略 (L3)
- [ ] **subject**【名】議題、件名、題目 (L2, R1)
- [ ] **switch**【動】入れ替わる (L3)
- [ ] **talk**【名】講演 (L3)
- [ ] **title**【名】題目 (L3)
- [ ] **traffic**【名】交通 (L3)

Vocabulary Check List

117

Unit 5　Personnel

- ☐ **accountant**【動】会計士 (R2)
- ☐ **affect**【動】影響を及ぼす (R1)
- ☐ **annual**【形】年に1度の (L4)
- ☐ **applicant**【名】志願者 (L3)
- ☐ **application form**【名】申し込み用紙　(R2)
- ☐ **apply for**【動】応募する (L2, L3)
- ☐ **assemble**【動】組み立てる (R3)
- ☐ **audience**【名】聴衆 (R1)
- ☐ **be disappointed at**
　　【動】〜にがっかりする (R1)
- ☐ **benefit**【名】給付金 (R3)
- ☐ **board member**【名】役員、取締役 (R1)
- ☐ **branch**【名】支店 (III)
- ☐ **brief**【形】短い (L4)
- ☐ **CEO**【名】最高経営責任者 (L4)
- ☐ **clerk**【名】事務員 (L3)
- ☐ **client**【名】顧客 (R1)
- ☐ **detail**【名】詳細 (R3)
- ☐ **earthquake**【名】地震 (R1)
- ☐ **electronic part**【名】電子部品 (R3)
- ☐ **equipment**【名】機器 (R3)
- ☐ **experienced**【形】経験のある (R3)
- ☐ **factory worker**【名】工場労働者 (R3)
- ☐ **fill out**【動】記入する (L2, L3)
- ☐ **full price**【名】全額 (Practice)
- ☐ **full-time position**【名】常勤職 (L3, R3)
- ☐ **hourly**【副】1時間ごとに (R3)
- ☐ **human resources**【名】人事部 (L2)
- ☐ **include**【動】含む (R3)
- ☐ **industry**【名】産業 (R1, R3)
- ☐ **inexperienced**【形】経験のない (R3)
- ☐ **inspect**【動】検査する (R3)
- ☐ **interviewee**【名】面接を受ける人 (L1)
- ☐ **interviewer**【名】面接官 (L1, L3)
- ☐ **introduce**【動】紹介する (L4)
- ☐ **laptop computer**
　　【名】ノート型パソコン (Grammar)
- ☐ **medical insurance**【名】医療保険 (R3)
- ☐ **mobile phone**【名】携帯電話 (L4)

- ☐ **offer**【動】提供する (R1)
- ☐ **open**【形】公募の(L3)
- ☐ **paid vacation**【名】有給休暇 (R3)
- ☐ **part-time job**【名】パートの仕事 (L2)
- ☐ **part-timer**【名】パート従業員 (L3)
- ☐ **personnel manager**【名】人事部長 (L4)
- ☐ **position**【名】地位 (L3, R1)
- ☐ **product**【名】製品 (Practice, R3)
- ☐ **profit**【名】売上利益 (Grammar)
- ☐ **prohibit**【動】禁止する (Practice)
- ☐ **refund**【動】払い戻しをする (Practice)
- ☐ **responsibility**【名】責任 (R3)
- ☐ **résumé**【名】履歴書 (L1, L3)
- ☐ **return**【動】戻す (R1)
- ☐ **schedule change**【名】予定変更 (R2)
- ☐ **ship**【動】配送する (R3)
- ☐ **sort**【動】仕分けする (R3)
- ☐ **switch on**【動】電源を入れる (L4)
- ☐ **turn off**【動】切る　(L4)
- ☐ **wage**【名】給料 (R3)

Unit 6　Shopping

- ☐ **a wide variety of ~**　多種多様な (6)
- ☐ **adjustable**【形】調整できる (7)
- ☐ **bookstore**【名】本屋 (3)
- ☐ **break**【名】休み、休憩（時間）(5)
- ☐ **break room**【名】休憩室 (5)
- ☐ **check out**【動】調べる (2)
- ☐ **clothes**【名】衣服 (2)
- ☐ **clothing**【名】服 (6)
- ☐ **clothing store**【名】洋服屋 (3)
- ☐ **colleague**【名】同僚 (Grammar)
- ☐ **conductor**【名】車掌 (3)
- ☐ **conference**【名】会議、協議会 (5)
- ☐ **construction site**【名】工事現場 (1)
- ☐ **cost**【動】（費用などが）かかる (7)
- ☐ **coupon**【名】優待券 (6)
- ☐ **description**【名】品目 (7)
- ☐ **delay**【名】遅れ (6)
- ☐ **delivery**【名】配達 (6)
- ☐ **due**【名】当然支払われるべきもの (7)
- ☐ **enter**【動】入る、入力する (1, 6)
- ☐ **entire**【形】全体の (5)
- ☐ **experience**【名】経験 (6)
- ☐ **expire**【動】失効する (6)
- ☐ **fall down**【動】転倒する、転ぶ (Grammar)
- ☐ **hurt**【動】傷つける (5)
- ☐ **invoice**【名】請求書 (7)
- ☐ **item**【名】商品 (4)
- ☐ **laptop computer**【名】ノート型パソコン (2)
- ☐ **look for**【動】~を探す (3)
- ☐ **mark down**【動】値下げする (4)
- ☐ **midnight**【名】真夜中、午前零時 (4)
- ☐ **offer**【名】提供 (6)
- ☐ **plan**【動】計画する (5)
- ☐ **price**【名】値段 (7)
- ☐ **purchase**【名】購入 (6)
- ☐ **quantity**【名】数量 (7)
- ☐ **reply**【動】返事する (5)
- ☐ **shelf**【名】棚 (2)
- ☐ **ship**【動】配送する (7)

- ☐ **shop clerk**【名】店員 (3)
- ☐ **subtotal**【名】小計 (7)
- ☐ **suggest**【動】提案する (6)
- ☐ **supplies**【名】商品、用品 (7)
- ☐ **total due**【名】受取総額、当然受け取るべき 合計金額 (7)
- ☐ **treadmill**【名】ルームランナー (7)
- ☐ **unit price**【名】単価 (7)
- ☐ **vote**【動】投票する (6)
- ☐ **wear**【名】衣類、衣服 (3)
- ☐ **weight**【名】ウェイトトレーニングの道具 (7)

Vocabulary Check List

Unit 7　Advertisement

- ☐ **a wide selection of** ～の幅広い品揃え (7)
- ☐ **ad**【名】広告 (2)
- ☐ **add up**【動】計算をする (2)
- ☐ **advertise**【動】広告する、宣伝する (2)
- ☐ **advertisement**【名】広告 (4)
- ☐ **analyze**【動】分析する (Grammar)
- ☐ **appear**【動】掲載される (7)
- ☐ **appliance store**【名】家庭用電気器具店 (6)
- ☐ **available**【形】入手可能な (6)
- ☐ **be after** 追う (Grammar)
- ☐ **be on sale** 特価で売出し中の (1)
- ☐ **be ready to do** ～する準備ができている (7)
- ☐ **beverage**【名】飲み物 (4)
- ☐ **brochure**【名】パンフレット、冊子 (3)
- ☐ **business hours**【名】営業時間 (7)
- ☐ **business trip**【名】出張 (7)
- ☐ **carry around**【動】持ち歩く (4)
- ☐ **cater for**【動】～のケータリングを引き受ける (7)
- ☐ **catering**【名】出前、ケータリング (7)
- ☐ **classified ad**【名】求人広告 (1)
- ☐ **come in**
  【動】～の形で売られる（提供される）(6)
- ☐ **competitor**【名】競争相手 (3)
- ☐ **computer screen**【名】コンピューターの画面 (1)
- ☐ **convenient**【形】便利な (4)
- ☐ **criminal**【名】犯人 (5)
- ☐ **customer**【名】顧客 (2)
- ☐ **delicious**【形】おいしい (7)
- ☐ **dishwasher**【名】食洗機 (6)
- ☐ **dishwashing**【名】食器洗い (6)
- ☐ **economic**【形】経済の (Grammar)
- ☐ **economics**【名】経済学 (Grammar)
- ☐ **engineer**【名】技師、エンジニア (Practice)
- ☐ **equipment**【名】器具 (5)
- ☐ **essential**【形】欠くことのできない (4)
- ☐ **flavor**【名】味わい、風味 (4)
- ☐ **furniture**【名】家具 (Grammar)
- ☐ **get a discount**【動】割引を受ける (7)
- ☐ **go with**【動】～によく合う (4)

- ☐ **grand-opening sale**【名】開店大売出し (2)
- ☐ **healthy**【形】健康的な (4)
- ☐ **hire**【動】雇う (3)
- ☐ **instant meal**【名】インスタント食品 (4)
- ☐ **job interview**【名】仕事の面接 (7)
- ☐ **kitchen equipment**【名】台所用品 (5)
- ☐ **labor cost**【名】人件費 (5)
- ☐ **mathematics**【名】数学 (5)
- ☐ **move-out day**
  【名】転出日、引っ越していく日 (7)
- ☐ **nutritional value**
  【名】栄養的価値、栄養価 (4)
- ☐ **occasion**【名】機会、場合 (7)
- ☐ **presentation**【名】発表 (5)
- ☐ **product**【名】商品 (4)
- ☐ **provide**【動】提供する (7)
- ☐ **rack**【名】棚、ラック (6)
- ☐ **reasonable**【形】（値段が）それほど高くない、
  手ごろな (4)
- ☐ **receive**【動】受け取る (7)
- ☐ **regular price**【名】通常価格 (1)
- ☐ **release**【動】新発売する (6)
- ☐ **search for**【動】～を探す (5)
- ☐ **shopper**【名】買い物客 (1)
- ☐ **similar**【形】似ている (3)
- ☐ **social science**
  【名】社会学、社会科学 (Grammar)
- ☐ **subject**【名】教科 (Practice)
- ☐ **supplement**【名】栄養補助食品 (4)
- ☐ **tag**【名】値札 (1)
- ☐ **trend**【名】動向 (Grammar)
- ☐ **vending machine**【名】自動販売機 (4)
- ☐ **warranty**【名】保証 (6)
- ☐ **washing machine**【名】洗濯機 (6)

Unit 8　Daily Life

- ☐ **administration**【名】管理局 (6)
- ☐ **at discounted price** 割引価格で (Practice)
- ☐ **auditorium**【名】ホール、講堂 (5)
- ☐ **battery**【名】電池 (3)
- ☐ **begin with**【動】〜から始まる (5)
- ☐ **borrow**【動】借りる (7)
- ☐ **brush**【動】はけで塗る (1)
- ☐ **bucket**【名】バケツ (1)
- ☐ **chain**【名】チェーン (6)
- ☐ **chance**【名】確率 (4)
- ☐ **check out**【動】借りる (7)
- ☐ **clean**【動】掃除する (1)
- ☐ **clear**【形】澄んだ (4)
- ☐ **cloudy**【形】曇った (4)
- ☐ **commentator**【名】解説者 (4)
- ☐ **complaint**【名】不平 (6)
- ☐ **complete**【動】完了する (6)
- ☐ **contact**【動】連絡を取る (6)
- ☐ **cool down**【動】冷え込む (4)
- ☐ **deadline**【名】締め切り (6)
- ☐ **degree**【名】（温度の単位の）度 (4)
- ☐ **delay**【名】遅れ、延滞 (7)
- ☐ **desktop computer**
　　【名】デスクトップパソコン (3)
- ☐ **discounted price**【名】割引価格 (Practice)
- ☐ **electronics store**【名】電気店 (3)
- ☐ **enclose**【動】同封する (7)
- ☐ **fail to do**【動】〜することを怠る (7)
- ☐ **farewell party**【名】送別会 (5)
- ☐ **fill in**【動】記入する (3)
- ☐ **film director**【名】映画監督 (4)
- ☐ **fine**【名】罰金 (7)
- ☐ **fragile**【形】壊れやすい (3)
- ☐ **further**【形】さらなる (7)
- ☐ **head**【名】長 (7)
- ☐ **high**【名】最高気温 (4)
- ☐ **inform**【動】知らせる (7)
- ☐ **instead**【副】代わりに (7)
- ☐ **laptop computer**【名】ノート型パソコン (3)

- ☐ **librarian**【名】図書館司書 (7)
- ☐ **lose**【動】紛失する (7)
- ☐ **low**【名】最低気温 (4)
- ☐ **make up one's mind**【動】決心する (2)
- ☐ **membership**
　　【名】会員であること、会員の身分 (7)
- ☐ **mobile phone**【名】携帯電話 (3)
- ☐ **move out**【動】引っ越しをする (7)
- ☐ **nearby**【副】すぐ近くに (7)
- ☐ **no longer** もはや〜ない (7)
- ☐ **not at all** 全く〜ない (2)
- ☐ **occupation**【名】職業、仕事 (4)
- ☐ **overdue**【形】期日を過ぎた (7)
- ☐ **ownership**【名】所有権、所有者 (6)
- ☐ **package**【名】小包 (3, 7)
- ☐ **paint**【名】絵具 (1)
- ☐ **place**【動】置く (1)
- ☐ **recipe**【名】料理法、レシピ (1)
- ☐ **remind**【動】気づかせる、思い出させる (7)
- ☐ **replacement**【名】交換の品 (7)
- ☐ **replacement fee**【名】交換費用 (7)
- ☐ **resident**【名】居住者 (6)
- ☐ **return**【動】戻る、返却する (2, 7)
- ☐ **right away** すぐに (7)
- ☐ **right now** 現時点では (4)
- ☐ **scientist**【名】科学者 (4)
- ☐ **serve**【動】（食事などを）出す (1)
- ☐ **shipment**【名】配送 (Practice)
- ☐ **spray bottle**【名】噴霧ボトル (1)
- ☐ **temperature**【名】気温 (4)
- ☐ **the day after tomorrow** 明後日 (4)
- ☐ **turn down**【動】〜を下げる、低くする (2)
- ☐ **turn off**【動】〜のスイッチを切る (2)
- ☐ **turn on**【動】〜のスイッチを入れる (2)
- ☐ **weather forecast**【名】天気予報 (2)
- ☐ **weather forecaster**【名】気象予報士 (4)
- ☐ **weather report**【名】天気予報 (4)

Unit 9   Office Work

- [ ] **across**【前】〜を横切って (4)
- [ ] **apply for**【動】〜に応募する (7)
- [ ] **appointment**【名】約束 (7)
- [ ] **assistant manager**【名】係長 (5)
- [ ] **badge**【名】バッジ、ID カード (4)
- [ ] **be located**【動】位置する (4)
- [ ] **be on duty** 勤務時間中で (4)
- [ ] **be promoted to**【動】〜に昇格する (5)
- [ ] **caller**【名】電話をかける人 (3)
- [ ] **convenient**【形】便利な、都合のよい (3)
- [ ] **customer**【名】客、顧客 (Grammar)
- [ ] **deadline**【名】締め切り (7)
- [ ] **desire to do**【動】〜することを望む (Practice)
- [ ] **drop by**【動】〜に立ち寄る (3)
- [ ] **employee**【名】従業員 (6)
- [ ] **empty**【形】空の (1)
- [ ] **establish**【動】確立する (Practice)
- [ ] **expand**【動】拡大する (Practice)
- [ ] **extend**【動】延長する (6)
- [ ] **extended hours**【名】時間延長 (6)
- [ ] **fingerprint**【名】指紋 (4)
- [ ] **fix**【動】修理する (2)
- [ ] **front office**【名】(顧客) 窓口部門 (7)
- [ ] **funding**【名】財政的支援、資金調達 (7)
- [ ] **furniture**【名】家具 (1)
- [ ] **guard**【名】警備員 (4)
- [ ] **in regards to** 〜に関して (7)
- [ ] **inform …of 〜**【動】…に〜の事柄を知らせる(7)
- [ ] **institution**【名】施設、協会、機関 (7)
- [ ] **jam**【動】詰まらせる (2)
- [ ] **lab equipment**【名】実験室備品 (7)
- [ ] **make copies**【動】コピーを取る (2)
- [ ] **memorandum**【名】メモ、覚書 (7)
- [ ] **newspaper stand**【名】新聞の売店 (1)
- [ ] **overtime**【形】時間外の (6)
- [ ] **overtime payment**【名】残業手当 (6)
- [ ] **parking area**【名】駐車場 (4)
- [ ] **payment**【名】支払い (6)
- [ ] **project**【名】企画 (7)

- [ ] **public image**
      【名】世間体、大衆イメージ (Practice)
- [ ] **receive**【動】受け取る (6)
- [ ] **refuse to do**
      【動】〜することを拒む (Grammar)
- [ ] **requirement**【名】要求 (7)
- [ ] **secretary**【名】秘書 (7)
- [ ] **security gate**【名】防犯ゲート (4)
- [ ] **supervisor**【名】監督者 (5)
- [ ] **wallet**【名】財布 (4)
- [ ] **weekday**【名】平日 (6)
- [ ] **weekend**【名】週末 (6)
- [ ] **work**【動】正常に機能する (2)
- [ ] **wristwatch**【名】腕時計 (1)

Unit 10　Business

- ☐ **aim to do**【動】〜することを目指す (7)
- ☐ **announce**【動】公表する (4)
- ☐ **attractive**【形】魅力的な (7)
- ☐ **be expected to do** 〜することになっている (4)
- ☐ **be ready to do** 〜する用意ができている (6)
- ☐ **calculator**【名】計算機 (1)
- ☐ **complete**【動】完了する (4)
- ☐ **construction**【名】工事 (4)
- ☐ **contract**【名】契約書 (3)
- ☐ **cost**【名】経費 (5)
- ☐ **deal with**【動】〜に対処する (5)
- ☐ **decline**【名】減少、衰退、落ち込み (7)
- ☐ **demand**【名】需要 (5)
- ☐ **document**【名】書類 (1)
- ☐ **enhanced**【形】改良された (7)
- ☐ **entirely**【副】完全に (7)
- ☐ **establish**【動】確立する (Practice)
- ☐ **expand**【動】拡大する (7)
- ☐ **factory**【名】工場 (4)
- ☐ **falling**【形】低迷している (7)
- ☐ **feature**【動】特色となる (7)
- ☐ **filing cabinet**【名】書類整理棚 (3)
- ☐ **findings**【名】研究結果 (6)
- ☐ **follow-up**【形】後に続く (7)
- ☐ **food chain**【名】食品チェーン店 (Practice)
- ☐ **glue**【名】接着剤、糊 (6)
- ☐ **gym**【名】体育館 (3)
- ☐ **increase**【動】増やす (7)
- ☐ **kit**【名】一式、セット (6)
- ☐ **laptop computer**【名】ノート型パソコン (1)
- ☐ **launch**【動】販売を開始する、始める (6)
- ☐ **leave**【動】残す (2)
- ☐ **leave for**【動】〜に向かって出発する (2)
- ☐ **limit**【動】制限する (7)
- ☐ **look over**【動】〜にざっと目を通す (3)
- ☐ **lunch break**【名】昼休み (3)
- ☐ **make an appointment**【動】約束をする (2)
- ☐ **maker**【名】メーカー (4)
- ☐ **market share**【名】市場占有率 (7)
- ☐ **messy**【形】散らかった (2)
- ☐ **plant**【名】工場 (4)
- ☐ **previous**【形】以前の (6)
- ☐ **previously**【副】以前に、これまでに (7)
- ☐ **product development team**
　　【名】商品開発チーム (6)
- ☐ **product manager**【名】製品管理者 (6)
- ☐ **put off**【動】延期する (5)
- ☐ **quality**【名】品質 (5)
- ☐ **report**【動】報告する、報じる (6, 7)
- ☐ **respond**【動】返答する (7)
- ☐ **responsibility**【名】責任 (5)
- ☐ **rubber band**【名】輪ゴム (4)
- ☐ **sacrifice**【動】犠牲にする (5)
- ☐ **sales department**【名】営業部 (2)
- ☐ **set up**【動】準備する (5)
- ☐ **unexpected**【形】予想外の (7)
- ☐ **urban**【形】都会の (Practice)

Unit 11 Traffic

- [ ] **absolute must**【名】至上命令 (6)
- [ ] **agenda**【名】議題 (5)
- [ ] **agenda item**【名】議案 (5)
- [ ] **announce**【動】公表する (5)
- [ ] **attend**【動】出席する (5)
- [ ] **board member**【名】役員、取締役 (5)
- [ ] **car accident**【名】自動車事故 (4)
- [ ] **completely**【副】完全に (4)
- [ ] **confusing**【形】混乱する (7)
- [ ] **construction**【名】工事 (4)
- [ ] **crowded**【形】混雑している (7)
- [ ] **damaged**【形】損害を受けた (4)
- [ ] **day off**【名】（平日に取る）休み (5)
- [ ] **downtown**【名】繁華街、中心街 (2)
- [ ] **driver's license**【名】運転免許証 (3)
- [ ] **due to** ～によって、～が原因で (4)
- [ ] **extra**【形】追加の (5)
- [ ] **fine**【名】罰金、【動】罰金を科する (6)
- [ ] **firefighter**【名】消防士 (3)
- [ ] **get off**【動】（乗り物など）から降りる (1)
- [ ] **give ~ a ride**【動】（人を）車に乗せる (2)
- [ ] **heavy**【形】いっぱいの、多い (1)
- [ ] **heavy snow**【名】大雪 (4)
- [ ] **inspect**【動】検査する (6)
- [ ] **inspection**【名】検査 (6)
- [ ] **local**【形】地元の、地方の (5)
- [ ] **make**【名】メーカー、製造者 (7)
- [ ] **mechanic**【名】機械工 (6)
- [ ] **move on to**【動】～に移る (5)
- [ ] **no-parking zone**【名】駐車禁止区域 (3)
- [ ] **newcomer**【名】新人、新入社員 (Practice)
- [ ] **occupation**【名】職業、仕事 (3)
- [ ] **overall**【副】全体で (7)
- [ ] **performance**【名】性能 (7)
- [ ] **police officer**【名】警察官 (3)
- [ ] **promise**【動】約束する (3)
- [ ] **punish**【動】罰する (6)
- [ ] **rank**【動】順位を占める (7)
- [ ] **rapid**【形】急速な (7)
- [ ] **reduce**【動】減らす (4)
- [ ] **regular**【形】定期的な (6)
- [ ] **reminder**【名】催促状、再通知 (6)
- [ ] **retire**【動】辞める (5)
- [ ] **right**【形】正しい、適切な (7)
- [ ] **seminar**【名】研修 (5)
- [ ] **session**【名】集まり (Practice)
- [ ] **speeding**【名】スピード違反 (3)
- [ ] **speeding ticket**【名】スピード違反切符 (3)
- [ ] **speed limit**【名】制限速度 (3)
- [ ] **sticker**【名】ステッカー (6)
- [ ] **test**【動】テストする (7)
- [ ] **ticket agent**【名】切符販売業者 (3)
- [ ] **traffic accident**【名】交通事故 (1)
- [ ] **traffic jam**【名】交通渋滞 (4, 7)
- [ ] **under construction** 工事中で (4)
- [ ] **up to** 最高～まで (6)
- [ ] **update**【名】最新情報 (4)

Unit 12 Finance and Banking

- [ ] **account**【名】口座 (6)
- [ ] **advantage**【名】有利な点 (7)
- [ ] **amount**【名】額 (6)
- [ ] **auction**【名】オークション (5)
- [ ] **bank account**【名】銀行口座 (3)
- [ ] **bank loan**【名】銀行ローン (7)
- [ ] **bank transfer**【名】銀行振替 (7)
- [ ] **banking**【名】銀行 (6)
- [ ] **below**【前】下の (7)
- [ ] **branch**【名】支店 (6)
- [ ] **calculator**【名】計算機 (1)
- [ ] **change**【名】つり銭、小銭 (2)
- [ ] **check**【名】小切手 (7)
- [ ] **click**【動】クリックする (7)
- [ ] **complain**【動】苦情を言う (4)
- [ ] **confuse**【動】混乱させる (7)
- [ ] **connect to**【動】〜に連絡する (4)
- [ ] **count**【動】数える (1)
- [ ] **earn**【動】稼ぐ (5)
- [ ] **effective**【形】効果的な (7)
- [ ] **enroll**【動】名前を登録する (7)
- [ ] **experienced**【形】経験を積んだ (7)
- [ ] **fill out**【動】記入する (2, 7)
- [ ] **financial consultant**
  【名】財政コンサルタント (7)
- [ ] **guarantee**【動】保証する (7)
- [ ] **guaranteed**【形】保証された (7)
- [ ] **heavy traffic**【名】交通渋滞 (5)
- [ ] **hold**【動】電話を切らずに待つ (4)
- [ ] **increase**【動】増加する (5)
- [ ] **inquiry**【名】問い合わせ (6)
- [ ] **invest**【動】投資する (7)
- [ ] **investment**【名】投資 (7)
- [ ] **investor**【名】投資家 (7)
- [ ] **last**【動】続く (Grammar)
- [ ] **line**【名】列 (1)
- [ ] **make a complaint**【動】苦情を言う (4)
- [ ] **matter**【名】事柄, 問題 (6)
- [ ] **navigate**【動】操る (7)

- [ ] **note**【名】紙幣 (2)
- [ ] **on one's own** 自分自身で (7)
- [ ] **out of order** 故障中で (3)
- [ ] **participant**【名】参加者 (7)
- [ ] **payment method**【名】支払方法 (7)
- [ ] **pension**【名】年金 (7)
- [ ] **register**【動】登録する (7)
- [ ] **report**【動】報告する (4)
- [ ] **representative**【名】担当者、代表者 (4)
- [ ] **sales manager**【名】営業部長 (5)
- [ ] **service representative**
  【名】サービス担当者 (4)
- [ ] **satisfaction**【名】満足 (7)
- [ ] **save**【動】蓄える (2)
- [ ] **save money**【動】貯金する (2)
- [ ] **savings**【名】貯蓄 (7)
- [ ] **savings account**【名】普通預金口座 (2)
- [ ] **seminar**【名】研修 (7)
- [ ] **side by side** 並んで (1)
- [ ] **simple**【形】簡単な (7)
- [ ] **stock market**【名】株式市場 (7)
- [ ] **ticket gate**【名】改札口 (3)
- [ ] **To whom it may concern**
  関係者各位、担当者の方へ (6)
- [ ] **transfer**【動】送金する (3, 6)
- [ ] **withdraw**【動】（預金を）引き出す (3)

Vocabulary Check List

Unit 13　Media

- [ ] **accomplishment**【名】達成 (7)
- [ ] **account**【名】アカウント (7)
- [ ] **ad-free**【形】広告掲載のない (7)
- [ ] **affordable**【形】手ごろな価格で (7)
- [ ] **ahead of**〜の前に (3)
- [ ] **await**【動】待つ (7)
- [ ] **announce**【動】公表する (4)
- [ ] **awesome**【形】驚くばかりの (7)
- [ ] **bazaar**【名】バザー (6)
- [ ] **below**【副】下に
- [ ] **be responsible for**〜に責任がある (4, 5)
- [ ] **browse**【動】ざっと見る、閲覧する (6)
- [ ] **check out**【動】調べる、確認する (6)
- [ ] **computer programmer**
      【名】コンピュータ・プログラマー (3)
- [ ] **contact number**【名】連絡先の番号 (3)
- [ ] **damaged product**【名】欠陥商品、破損品 (5)
- [ ] **day off**【名】（平日に取る）休み (5)
- [ ] **decision**【名】決定、決意 (4)
- [ ] **decrease**【動】減らす (4)
- [ ] **device**【名】機器 (7)
- [ ] **disappear**【動】消滅する (7)
- [ ] **distant**【形】遠い (7)
- [ ] **evaluation**【名】評価 (5)
- [ ] **extensive**【形】広範囲に及ぶ (7)
- [ ] **favorite**【形】一番好きな (7)
- [ ] **financial**【形】財政上の (4)
- [ ] **fix**【動】修理する (3)
- [ ] **flight attendant**【名】客室乗務員 (4)
- [ ] **go online**【動】インターネットに接続する (6)
- [ ] **hard copy**
      【名】ハードコピー、プリントアウトした紙 (6)
- [ ] **in no hurry**急がないで、焦らないで (3)
- [ ] **informative**【形】有益な (Practice)
- [ ] **international flight**【名】国際線 (4)
- [ ] **issue**【名】（定期刊行物の）号 (2)
- [ ] **journey**【名】旅 (7)
- [ ] **lay off**【動】解雇する (4)
- [ ] **lend**【動】貸す (2)

- [ ] **limted**【形】限定された (7)
- [ ] **make payment**【動】支払いをする (7)
- [ ] **major**【形】主な (3)
- [ ] **million**【名】百万　(7)
- [ ] **musical instrument**【名】楽器 (7)
- [ ] **news stand**【名】新聞の売店 (2)
- [ ] **offer**【動】提供する (6)
- [ ] **office manager**
      【名】業務マネージャー、事務長 (5)
- [ ] **official**【名】職員、当局者 (4)
- [ ] **offline**【形】オフラインで (7)
- [ ] **order**【名】注文 (5)
- [ ] **past**【名】昔、過去(7)
- [ ] **plumber**【名】配管工 (3)
- [ ] **process**【動】処理する (5)
- [ ] **proud**【形】自慢して、誇って (7)
- [ ] **publication**【名】刊行物、出版物 (6)
- [ ] **rank 〜 as …**【動】〜を…と位置付ける(7)
- [ ] **rapidly**【副】急速に (7)
- [ ] **rare**【形】まれな、珍しい (7)
- [ ] **real estate agent**【名】不動産業者 (3)
- [ ] **remote control**【名】リモコン (1)
- [ ] **rent**【名】賃貸料 (2)
- [ ] **repairperson**【名】修理工 (3)
- [ ] **retailer**【名】小売業者、小売店　(5)
- [ ] **save**【動】蓄える (Practice)
- [ ] **source**【名】情報源、源 (7)
- [ ] **stand in line**行列を作る (2)
- [ ] **subscription**【名】定期購読 (6)
- [ ] **upside down**【名】逆さまに (1)
- [ ] **within**【前】〜以内に (5)

Unit 14　Health and Welfare

- [ ] **act as**【動】～の役をつとめる (7)
- [ ] **appearance**【名】出現、外見(6)
- [ ] **attractive**【形】魅力的な (5)
- [ ] **available**【形】利用可能な (7)
- [ ] **availability**【名】利用できること (4)
- [ ] **be fined**【動】罰金が科される (2)
- [ ] **be sure to do** 必ず～する (6)
- [ ] **branch manager**【名】支店長 (Practice)
- [ ] **brochure**【名】冊子、パンフレット(5)
- [ ] **bulletin board**【名】掲示板 (4)
- [ ] **competitive**【形】競争の激しい (5)
- [ ] **complete**【形】完成した (7)
- [ ] **contact**【動】連絡を取る
- [ ] **dental clinic**【名】歯科 (2)
- [ ] **enough**【形】十分な (3)
- [ ] **entrance**【名】入り口 (4)
- [ ] **exercise**【名】運動【動】運動をする (3, 4)
- [ ] **extension**【名】内線 (7)
- [ ] **facility**【名】施設 (7)
- [ ] **field**【名】分野 (5)
- [ ] **fingerprint**【名】指紋 (4)
- [ ] **fitness equipment**【名】フィットネス装置 (7)
- [ ] **fluently**【副】流暢に (Practice)
- [ ] **follow**【動】従う (3)
- [ ] **free of charge** 無料で (7)
- [ ] **get back**【動】戻る
- [ ] **get up**【動】起床する (3)
- [ ] **hold on to**【動】～をつかんで離さない、
　　　　　　　　～にしがみつく(1)
- [ ] **job postings**【名】求人 (5)
- [ ] **leave**【動】退職する (6)
- [ ] **make time for**【動】～のために時間を作る (3)
- [ ] **manual**【名】説明書 (Grammar)
- [ ] **medicine**【名】薬 (2)
- [ ] **notify**【動】知らせる、通知する (6)
- [ ] **off duty** 勤務時間外の、非番の (4)
- [ ] **on duty** 勤務中の (4)
- [ ] **on vacation** 休暇中で (6)
- [ ] **posting**【名】投稿 (5)

- [ ] **prefer**【動】好む (6)
- [ ] **provide**【動】提供する (7)
- [ ] **receptionist**【名】受付係 (4)
- [ ] **register**【動】登録する (4)
- [ ] **repair**【名】修理 (4)
- [ ] **request**【動】依頼する (6)
- [ ] **return**【動】戻る (6)
- [ ] **run**【動】続く (7)
- [ ] **search for**【動】～を探す (5)
- [ ] **slide**【名】すべり台 (1)
- [ ] **specialist**【名】専門医 (6)
- [ ] **storage**【名】物の保管場所 (7)
- [ ] **strength-training machine**
　　　　【名】筋力トレーニングマシーン (7)
- [ ] **suffer from**【動】～を患う、～に苦しむ (2)
- [ ] **take a walk**【動】散歩をする (3)
- [ ] **take advantage of**【動】～を利用する (7)
- [ ] **take care of**【動】～を世話をする (1)
- [ ] **talk into a microphone**
　　　　【動】マイクに向かって話す (1)
- [ ] **throw away**【動】捨てる (4)
- [ ] **treadmill**【名】ルームランナー (7)
- [ ] **useful**【形】使い勝手が良い (Grammar)

不規則動詞活用表

A-B-C 型（原形，過去形，過去分詞がすべて異なる形）

原形	過去形	過去分詞形	意味
be	was / were	been	～である
begin	began	begun	始める
break	broke	broken	壊す
choose	chose	chosen	選ぶ
do	did	done	する
draw	drew	drawn	描く
drink	drank	drunk	飲む
drive	drove	driven	運転する
eat	ate	eaten	食べる
fall	fell	fallen	落ちる
fly	flew	flown	飛ぶ
forget	forgot	forgotten	忘れる
get	got	gotten / got	得る
give	gave	given	与える
go	went	gone	行く
grow	grew	grown	成長する
hide	hid	hidden	隠す
know	knew	known	知っている
lie	lay	lain	横たわる
ride	rode	ridden	乗る
rise	rose	risen	上がる
see	saw	seen	見る
shake	shook	shaken	振る
show	showed	shown / showed	示す
sing	sang	sung	歌う
speak	spoke	spoken	話す
steal	stole	stolen	盗む
swim	swam	swum	泳ぐ
take	took	taken	取る
tear	tore	torn	裂く
throw	threw	thrown	投げる
wear	wore	worn	着ている
write	wrote	written	書く

A-A-A 型（原形，過去形，過去分詞がすべて同じ形）

原形	過去形	過去分詞形	意味
cost	cost	cost	費用がかかる
cut	cut	cut	切る
hit	hit	hit	叩く
hurt	hurt	hurt	傷つける
let	let	let	させる
put	put	put	置く

原形	過去形	過去分詞形	意味
quit	quit	quit	辞める
read	read	read	読む
set	set	set	置く
shut	shut	shut	閉じる

A-B-A 型（原形と過去分詞が同じ形）

原形	過去形	過去分詞形	意味
become	became	become	～になる
come	came	come	来る
run	ran	run	走る

A-B-B 型（過去形と過去分詞が同じ形）

原形	過去形	過去分詞形	意味
bring	brought	brought	持ってくる
build	built	built	建てる
buy	bought	bought	買う
catch	caught	caught	つかまえる
feel	felt	felt	感じる
find	found	found	見つける
have	had	had	持っている
hear	heard	heard	聞こえる
hold	held	held	持つ
keep	kept	kept	保つ
lay	laid	laid	横たえる
lead	led	led	導く
leave	left	left	立ち去る
lend	lent	lent	貸す
lose	lost	lost	なくす
make	made	made	作る
mean	meant	meant	意味する
meet	met	met	会う
pay	paid	paid	支払う
say	said	said	言う
sell	sold	sold	売る
send	sent	sent	送る
shoot	shot	shot	撃つ
shine	shone	shone	輝く
sit	sat	sat	座る
sleep	slept	slept	眠る
spend	spent	spent	費やす
stand	stood	stood	立つ
teach	taught	taught	教える
tell	told	told	話す
think	thought	thought	思う
understand	understood	understood	理解する
win	won	won	勝つ

不規則動詞活用表

129

新形式対応
ブリッジから始めるTOEIC® L&R テスト

検印
省略

©2021 年 1 月 31 日　第 1 版発行
2024 年 1 月 31 日　第 3 刷発行

編著者　　　　　　　　　　　　林　　姿穂
　　　　　　　　　　　　　　　西田　晴美
　　　　　　　　　　　　　　　Brian Covert

発行者　　　　　　　　　　　　小川　洋一郎
発行所　　　　　　　　　　株式会社 朝日出版社
　　　　　　　　〒101-0065 東京都千代田区西神田 3-3-5
　　　　　　　　　　　電話　東京　(03) 3239-0271
　　　　　　　　　　　FAX　東京　(03) 3239-0479
　　　　　　　　　e-mail　text-e@asahipress.com
　　　　　　　　　　　振替口座　00140-2-46008
　　　　　　　　　　　　www.asahipress.com
　　　　　　　組版／メディアアート　製版／錦明印刷

ISBN978-4-255-15667-5